THE FOOD & COOKING OF
PORTUGAL

THE FOOD & COOKING OF
PORTUGAL

TRADITIONS • INGREDIENTS • TASTES • TECHNIQUES • 65 CLASSIC RECIPES

MIGUEL CASTRO E SILVA
PHOTOGRAPHY BY WILLIAM LINGWOOD

This edition is published by Aquamarine, an imprint of Anness Publishing Ltd, Hermes House, 88–89 Blackfriars Road, London SE1 8HA; tel. 020 7401 2077; fax 020 7633 9499

www.aquamarinebooks.com; www.annesspublishing.com

If you like the images in this book and would like to investigate using them for publishing, promotions or advertising, please visit our website www.practicalpictures.com for more information.

UK agent: The Manning Partnership Ltd;
tel. 01225 478444; fax 01225 478440;
sales@manning-partnership.co.uk

UK distributor: Grantham Book Services Ltd;
tel. 01476 541080; fax 01476 541061;
orders@gbs.tbs-ltd.co.uk

North American agent/distributor:
National Book Network; tel. 301 459 3366;
fax 301 429 5746; www.nbnbooks.com

Australian agent/distributor: Pan Macmillan Australia; tel. 1300 135 113; fax 1300 135 103; customer.service@macmillan.com.au

New Zealand agent/distributor: David Bateman Ltd;
tel. (09) 415 7664; fax (09) 415 8892

Publisher: Joanna Lorenz
Senior Managing Editor: Conor Kilgallon
Project Editor: Emma Clegg
Concept Design: Simon Daley
Project Designer: Nigel Partridge
Illustrator: Robert Highton
Photography: William Lingwood
Food Stylist: Lucy McKelvie
Prop Stylist: Helen Trent
Production Controller: Claire Rae

© Anness Publishing Ltd 2007, 2008

A CIP catalogue record for this book is available from the British Library.

ETHICAL TRADING POLICY

At Anness Publishing we believe that business should be conducted in an ethical and ecologically sustainable way, with respect for the environment and a regard to the replacement of the natural resources we employ. As a publisher, we use a lot of wood pulp to make high-quality paper for printing, and that wood commonly comes from spruce trees. We are therefore currently growing more than 500,000 trees in two Scottish forest plantations near Aberdeen – Berrymoss (130 hectares/320 acres) and West Touxhill (125 hectares/305 acres). The forests we manage contain twice the number of trees employed each year in paper-making for our books.

Because of this ongoing ecological investment programme, you, as our customer, can have the pleasure and reassurance of knowing that a tree is being cultivated on your behalf to naturally replace the materials used to make the book you are holding.

Our forestry programme is run in accordance with the UK Woodland Assurance Scheme (UKWAS) and will be certified by the internationally recognized Forest Stewardship Council (FSC). The FSC is a non-government organization dedicated to promoting responsible management of the world's forests. Certification ensures forests are managed in an environmentally sustainable and socially responsible way. For further information about this scheme, go to www.annesspublishing.com/trees.

NOTES

• Bracketed terms are intended for American readers.
• For all recipes, quantities are given in both metric and imperial measures and, where appropriate, in standard cups and spoons. Follow one set of measures, but not a mixture, because they are not interchangeable.
• Standard spoon and cup measures are level. 1 tsp = 5ml, 1 tbsp = 15ml, 1 cup = 250ml/8fl oz.
• Australian standard tablespoons are 20ml. Australian readers should use 3 tsp in place of 1 tbsp for measuring small quantities of gelatine, flour, salt, etc.
• American pints are 16fl oz/2 cups. American readers should use 20fl oz/2.5 cups in place of 1 pint when measuring liquids.
• Electric oven temperatures in this book are for conventional ovens. When using a fan oven, the temperature will probably need to be reduced by about 10–20°C/20–40°F. Since ovens vary, you should check with your manufacturer's instruction book for guidance.
• The nutritional analysis given for each recipe is calculated per portion (i.e. serving or item), unless otherwise stated. If the recipe gives a range, such as Serves 4–6, then the nutritional analysis will be for the smaller portion size, i.e. 6 servings. Measurements for sodium do not include salt added to taste.
• Medium (US large) eggs are used unless otherwise stated.

CONTENTS

GEOGRAPHY & LANDSCAPE

Portugal is a land of amazing variety. From the remote and mountainous region in the north to the crowded tourist beaches of the Algarve in the south, from the historic borders with Spain in the east to the wild Atlantic Ocean in the west, this small country accommodates many different kinds of climate, culture and cuisine. It can be divided roughly into three parts – northern, central and southern – each with its own identity and regional characteristics.

Portugal resembles an elongated rectangle standing on its short end, which is firmly planted in the Atlantic Ocean. On a map, it looks so close to North Africa that it seems amazing that Portugal was once thought of as the end of the civilized world. Its eastern and northern borders are bounded by Spain, but to the west and south there is nothing but thousands of miles of Atlantic Ocean between Portugal and the Americas.

Each of the three regions of Portugal (northern, central and southern) contains one of the major rivers of Portugal: the Douro rolls through the northern mountains; the mighty Tagus flows through the central region down to Lisbon; and the Guadiana meanders gently through the southern plains and into the sea on the border with Spain.

BELOW Sun-loving tourists from across the world are drawn to Portugal's warm waters, the sun-drenched beaches and the dramatic coastal scenery.

THE NORTHERN REGION

The Douro river in the north wends westwards through the rugged countryside to the coast at Porto. In this northern area, the landscape is surprisingly green; lush valleys nestle between the mountain peaks, and the prevailing winds from the Atlantic bring moderate rainfall and cold temperatures in the winter, but also sunny and warm weather in the summer.

The inland part of this region forms part of the ancient Iberian plateau, a region of Europe with its own culture and traditions. And the topography gives rise to a particular kind of agriculture. Livestock are particularly suited to this rugged terrain, and so meat figures largely in northern Portuguese dishes.

In the remote north-eastern countryside known as *Tras-os-Montes,* thick forests cover the mountain slopes. The trees growing here include chestnuts, almonds and olives; there are also steep terraced vineyards flourishing in the sunny foothills.

The northern region's coastline, where several smaller rivers flow down to the sea, is known as the Minho area, after the river that forms its boundary with Spain to the north. This part of the region is flatter and more suited to intensive agriculture, especially the cultivation of vines to make a slightly sparkling, fresh wine, *vinho verde.* On the coast, in the northern part of Portugal as well as the south, fishing ports grew up to harvest the abundant seafood of the Atlantic, and became important trading posts in the adventurous era of exploration in the 15th and 16th centuries. This was a time when many of the ingredients we think of as typically Portuguese were first brought to the country from far lands.

1 MINHO
2 TRÁS-OS-MONTES
3 DOURO
4 BEIRO
5 ESTREMADURA
6 RIBATEJO
7 ALENTEJO
8 THE ALGARVE

North Atlantic Ocean

PORTUGAL

SPAIN

Valença
Douro
Porto
Vila Real
Mondego
Guarda
Tagus
Castelo Branco
Santarém
Portalegre
Lisbon★
Setúbal
Guadiana
Beja
Santo António
Faro
Gulf of Cádiz

THE CENTRAL REGION

This section of Portugal is dominated by the Tagus river (Rio Tejo), whose long course ends at the capital city, Lisbon, where it finally joins the ocean. The Tagus, like the Douro, rises in the Spanish plateau, its waters fed by lakes and springs in the central Spanish mountains, and flows for 600 miles/965km before it meets the broad, flat alluvial plain of the coastal region. This central coastal area used to suffer frequent floods, but the flow is now better controlled by several dams further upriver in Spain. The Tagus river adds richness to the central part of Portugal by washing fertile soil down to the plains and irrigating the crops – wheat, barley and vines – that are grown in abundance there.

THE SOUTHERN REGION

Portugal's landscape flattens out further south below the Tagus estuary. From Lisbon to the south-western tip of the country at Cabo Sao Vincente, the climate is hotter and so this part is even more suitable for growing crops on a large scale. The third of Portugal's major rivers, the Guadiana, flows from north to south through this region.

The Algarve sits at the southern edge of Portugal and is its most popular tourist destination with its rocky cliffs, beautiful beaches and uninterrupted sunshine. Its climate is hot and dry, which means all sorts of exotic foods can be grown here, such as rice, citrus fruits, figs and almonds.

PORTUGAL'S ISLANDS

The Portuguese island groups of the Azores and the Madeira Islands are rich with their own cultures and traditions. These volcanic island archipelagos are geographically closer to Africa than mainland Europe and the subtropical climates that these islands enjoy are perfect for growing grapes, sugarcane and bananas.

REGIONAL IDENTITY

Communications between the coastal towns and the interior of Portugal have not been easy in past centuries. Mountains rise from the plains, with high, remote valleys and deep gorges, which were difficult to cross, and winter rains left tracks impassable. This meant that the different regions of Portugal kept their own identities and culinary traditions well into the 20th century. Cooks are proud of their regional culinary heritage and many families, in order to celebrate their history and traditions, still enjoy making a pilgrimage to a particular area where a local delicacy is served.

ABOVE LEFT Bordered only by Spain, Portugal is the western-most country of mainland Europe.

ABOVE RIGHT The mountainous Portuguese island of Madeira sits on a massive shield volcano, which last erupted over 6,500 years ago.

FESTIVALS & CELEBRATIONS

Portugal's rich cultural and religious heritage is reflected in the many festivals celebrated with great gusto throughout the year. Often, a festival's religious origins combine with a healthy attention to the food and drink associated with it: for example, the special cake eaten at Epiphany; bread and wine at the Festa dos Tabuleiros in July; chestnuts for Sao Martinho in the autumn. And of course, it is a great excuse for a party.

NEW YEAR

The celebrations for New Year start with special church services, and in the north of Portugal *janeiras* (New Year songs) are sung from door to door in return for money and food. People eat twelve grapes as the church bells strike midnight, which guarantees a happy twelve months ahead.

At Epiphany (6 January), a family feast is often held with a special ring-shaped cake containing small gifts for the children and, somewhere hidden within it, one dried broad bean. The lucky finder of the bean becomes king for the day, but has to promise to make the cake next year! This is a time for family treats and visits to relations, when wine and sweets are brought out and carols are sung in celebration of the birth of Christ.

BELOW Girls in traditional costume and flower headdresses at the Spring Flower Festival in Funchal, the capital of the Madeira islands.

On 22 January comes the festival of Sao Vicente, the patron saint of Lisbon. Farmers used to predict the year's harvest by carrying a lighted torch to the top of a hill; if it blew out, the harvest would be good, but if it stayed alight, a bad harvest would follow.

FEBRUARY

Before the restrictions of Lent begin on Ash Wednesday, carnivals are held in many Portuguese cities. Parties and dances are common throughout the country, and it's a time of licence when people act irresponsibly. Battles with eggs, flour and water used to take place, but these days the festivities are more likely to consist of parades and dressing up.

EASTER

As a country with a strong religious tradition, there are many Easter festivals. Starting on Palm Sunday and continuing throughout Holy Week, there are church processions around villages and towns. A *Folar* cake is made to celebrate Easter, decorated with hard-boiled eggs on top of a sweet dough.

WHITSUN

At Pentecost, special feasts are held, traditionally in aid of the poor. Tables covered with food are laid out in the street. The feasting can go on for eleven days until the religious festival of Corpus Christi, when major church celebrations take place. In Ponta Delgada on San Miguel, the procession passes over a long carpet of flower petals.

JUNE

Santo Antonio on 13 June sees more feasting, and children begging for pennies. The saint was born in Lisbon, and when the church of Santo Antonio was

destroyed in the Lisbon earthquake in 1755, the children collected money for its restoration. The money is now more likely to be spent on a party.

On 23 June, Saint John's Eve, there are rituals concerning love, health and fertility, with the burning of pine branches and the preservation of the ashes. The next day, Saint John's Day, brings a festival in Braga, in the northern province of Minho, which includes colourful parades, bullfights and fireworks, and the medieval Dance of King David.

Sao Pedro, the patron saint of fishermen, is celebrated on 29 June. The coastal towns and villages put on a good show, with fireworks, parades and dancing. It's an opportunity to try the local fish dishes, such as grilled sardines, oysters or fish stew.

JULY
The Festa Dos Tabuleiros is held in the central city of Tomar every other year. A thanksgiving festival for harvest time, food plays a major part alongside dancing, processions and other entertainments. Processions of girls wear flowers as well as small loaves of bread in their huge headdresses to symbolize the harvest. Bread, wine and meat are blessed by priests and then distributed to the poor.

AUGUST
On the first Sunday in August, the ancient town of Guimaraes celebrates its proud history as the birthplace of Portugal's first king, Dom Afonso Henriques. The noise of fairs, processions and fireworks can be deafening. Local bread and cakes

dominate the feasting – huge round loaves, little bread rolls in the shape of animals, and sugar-coated cakes and sweets are available on the street.

SEPTEMBER
Another fisherman's festival is held in Nazare each September. This is in honour of Our Lady of Nazare, where a chapel was built by Dom Fuas, a grateful hunter who had a sudden vision of the Virgin, which stopped him from falling over a cliff in thick fog. The local fishermen adopted the chapel as a centre of pilgrimage and give thanks for Our Lady's protection against the perils of the sea.

NOVEMBER
The dead are remembered on 1 November, All Saints' Day. In the past, food was taken into churchyards to eat; now open-air feasts are more likely to be held in the streets. The grown-ups drink wine and eat chestnuts, while the children prefer sugar cakes flavoured with cinnamon and herbs specially made for this day.

The traditional day for slaughtering the family pig falls on 11 November, the festival of Sao Martinho. The feasts include more wine and chestnuts, seasonal produce which goes very well with pork.

CHRISTMAS
The Portuguese love a family reunion, and this is a good excuse to eat and drink around a burning *cepo de Natal* (Yule log). Crumbs are left on the hearth or food on the table for wandering ghosts.

ABOVE LEFT Young men carry the image of a Madonna through Castelo Rodrigo during a feast-day celebration.

ABOVE RIGHT Dancing is a fundamental part of any Portuguese celebration, with each region proud of its own traditional costumes, music and movements.

PORTUGUESE WINE

Grapevines were first planted in Portugal during the Roman occupation, some 2,000 years ago, and wine production has since become a significant part of the economy. For such a small country, Portugal still punches way above its weight in the international wine trade, with its most famous wines, port and madeira, distributed globally – it is number six in the worldwide list of wine producers, a source of justifiable national pride.

WINES OF THE NORTH
In 1756 the Douro region, in the north, became the world's first demarcated wine production region. The famous *vinho do Porto*, port wine, is produced in the rugged Trás-os-Montes, with its special soil and weather conditions – hot in summer, cold in winter. The wines produced in the region were exported to various destinations, especially England, and were fortified for the long trip by ship. This fortifying technique has developed through the centuries to give the strong, fruity port wine that we know today. As they age, port wines develop an elegance and refinement which replaces the strength of their youth. There are two main types of port: ruby, which goes through the ageing process in the bottle and has an aroma of red berries; and tawny, which is matured in casks and is subject to a slight oxidation process, making it taste more of dried fruit.

Port is not the only wine made in the Douro region, however. It also produces top-quality table wines which are perfect for drinking with dinner. This wine is usually a deep red colour, and it keeps well.

Still in the far north of the country, a wonderful light wine called *vinho verde* ("green" or "fresh" wine) is produced, which has very little alcohol. This wine is made with Loureiro and Arinto grapes, which give *vinho verde* a fruity and citric aroma, balanced with an intense acidity. As it reaches the border with Spain, the Alvarinho grape produces a very elegant and well-structured wine with the aroma of exotic fruits.

WINES OF THE CENTRAL REGION
Central Portugal has two wine-producing regions: Dão and Bairrada. From the Dão region, the inland area, come superior wines

BELOW LEFT
A worker harvesting grapes in the rugged landscape of Trás-os-Montes to produce Portugal's famous port wine.

BELOW RIGHT Port is aged in wooden barrels. The process of oxidation and evaporation combined with exposure to the wooden casks is used to produce tawny port.

WINES OF PORTUGAL

Type	Region	Characteristics	When to drink
Port	Northern (Douro, inland)	Ruby or tawny, sweet fortified wine	With cheese and with some appetizers
Douro	Northern (Douro, inland)	Mainly red, intense and fruity Complex white wines	With red meat and game
Vinho verde	Northern (Minho, coastal)	Mainly white, slightly sparkling, low alcohol	With any food, particularly fish and seafood
Dão	Central	Mainly red and fruity	With any food, especially fish and white meat, or on its own
Bairrada	Central (coastal)	Red, strong, best matured	With any food
Bucelas	Central south	White, balanced and fresh	With fish and on its own
Moscatel	Central (coastal)	Tawny, dark and sweet	With dessert
Alentejo	Southern (plains)	Mainly red	With any food or on its own
Madeira	Island of Madeira	Tawny and sweet fortified wine, best matured	With dessert and for cooking

made from the Touriga Nacional grape, which gives a mature, intense aroma. Dão wine is very popular in every Portuguese home and restaurant. In the Bairrada region, where the climate is determined by the proximity of the sea, the local Baga grapes make wine with a high tannin content, and this wine needs to be kept for a while before drinking.

South of the River Tagus, near the sea in the Terras do Sado area, Castelão grapes are commonly grown in the sandy soil. This is the land where Moscatel wines are cultivated, which are strong and sweet, with a distinctive aroma of nuts and raisins. The coastal strip, Estremadura, from the Latin meaning "farthest land on the Douro", is also beginning to produce more high-quality wine, with the introduction of various modern cultivation methods.

WINES OF THE SOUTH

In the Alentejo, which is the flatter southern region between Lisbon and the Algarve, the vast plains allow for the widespread cultivation of grapes using the most up-to-date technology, and this method gives great consistency in quality. The intense summer heat in this area produces full-bodied reds and mature white wines.

MADEIRA

The island of Madeira, which has been a part of Portugal since the 15th century, has a long history of growing grapes. It produces the famous strong Madeira wine, which is still produced on the island using original methods. The main vineyards have a southern exposure and are at Câmara de Lôbos and Santana on the north coast. Madeira wine has a distinctive quality and a capacity to improve with age.

ABOVE Only grapes grown in Portugal's Douro region, the oldest defined and protected wine region in the world, go on to produce port.

PORTUGUESE CUISINE

Portugal is so rich in locally sourced ingredients that it has given great inspiration to the inventive cook over the centuries, ever since the Romans first marched here and stopped at the Atlantic Ocean, thinking it was the edge of the world. From pork ribs to prawns, from fresh sardines to sheep's cheese, from chestnuts to cabbage, Portuguese food is a riot of flavour and freshness, using everything this favourable climate can provide.

THE PORTUGUESE MEAL

Many Portuguese people consider food and drink to be one of the most important parts of their life. As in most other southern European countries, breakfast is a quick affair of coffee and rolls. Lunch takes longer, and often consists of one main course – in a restaurant, the *prato do dia* (dish of the day) is very popular with the locals. The serious eating of the day is in the evening; the Portuguese eat dinner around 7p.m. to 10p.m. (not as late as their Spanish neighbours), and this is the time for families to be together. Sunday lunch, with the extended family, is a big occasion which you skip at your peril. Even now, when Portugal is a thriving, modern European country, the family meal is still taken very seriously as a punctuation mark in the week.

One delightful tradition enjoyed by the Portuguese and their visitors in bars, cafés and restaurants is *petiscos*. These are delicious morsels of meat, fish or vegetables with bread and a glass or two of wine. The idea is somewhat similar to the Spanish *tapas* – it's a great way to have a taste of many different dishes, and give yourself plenty of time to socialize.

EXOTIC DISCOVERIES

Over the centuries, Portugal has had the good fortune to discover and grow many fine ingredients for cooking. Some of these were brought to the country by invading armies in the first millennium; others were imported by the explorers of the 15th and 16th centuries. When Vasco da Gama opened the sea route to India in 1498, he provided Portuguese cooks with some of their favourite ingredients, which are still used today – cinnamon, coriander, cumin, paprika and cloves. A few years later, even more trading routes were opened to Brazil and Africa, giving the Portuguese access to nuts, beans, coffee and the tiny chilli pepper which makes a fiery Portuguese favourite, piri-piri sauce. It is the combination of these more exotic ingredients with the natural abundance of fresh fish, seafood, locally grown meat and aromatic herbs from the hillsides that makes Portuguese cuisine so rich and fresh.

While spices and chilli peppers may give flavour, they cannot, on their own, fill the stomach, so a good solid base was needed to keep the hungry farmers and fishermen satisfied. Luckily, the Moors brought them rice from North Africa, which flourishes in the warm climate of the Algarve; potatoes and tomatoes came over from the New

BELOW Mealtimes in Portugal are a regular celebration of family life, with gatherings around the dinner table lasting many hours.

World; and wheat for bread-making is a major crop in the plains south of Lisbon. Potatoes or rice form the basis of many dishes, eking out a small amount of fish or meat; and, as with all other southern European cuisines, there is the tomato. The Portuguese stew *feijoada* is based on beans originally grown in Brazil, combined with meat and vegetables. Naturally, bread mops up all those wonderful juices so that nothing is wasted. It is even used as an ingredient in some soups.

NATIVE FAVOURITES

Traditionally, Portuguese cooks have had to be both frugal and resourceful in making full use of native animals for food, particularly the pig. Farmers and smallholders knew how to use every part of a pig so that the meat from one animal lasted a family through the cold winter days. They still make all kinds of sausages, *morcela* (a spicy black pudding made with pig's blood) and cured ham, as well as eating the main pork cuts when they are fresh. The pig is a fantastically productive animal and a Portuguese favourite.

Other popular dishes are based on lamb, goat and poultry, also ideal animals to keep in the rocky, inland areas of the country, where crops such as wheat cannot be grown on a viable scale.

Around the coast, of course, fish and seafood are the main ingredients. Many a Portuguese *caldeirada* (fish stew) is based on large amounts of vegetables with white wine and whatever fish is available. The cod caught by Portuguese fishermen far away in the cold waters of the North Atlantic used to be salted to preserve it until they arrived back. This has become such a favourite that *bacalhau* (salt cod) is known as "the faithful friend".

COOKING TECHNIQUES

The Portuguese like to use fresh ingredients. When they are eating fresh fish or meat, it is likely to be simply grilled (broiled) or baked; however, the need to eke out small amounts of protein with large amounts of starch and vegetables means that there are many Portuguese recipes for soups, stews and casseroles. These dishes can combine fish and meat with rice, potatoes or other vegetables, in a sauce of tomatoes, garlic and wine. They tend to be cooked at low temperatures for a long time.

When the Moors invaded Portugal, over a thousand years ago, they brought a special cooking pan called a *cataplana*, a kind of pressure cooker, which steams the food to make it tender. The dish looks like two woks clipped together, with a rounded base and a rounded lid to seal in the flavour, and is often made of copper or bronze. If you would like to try this method of cooking you can buy a *cataplana* from specialist suppliers.

LEFT An elderly woman preparing corn at Fajã Grande, a parish in the municipality of Lajes das Flores in the Azores.

BELOW A couple dining at a restaurant at Castelo de São Jorge, a hilltop citadel with spectacular views over Lisbon.

REGIONAL DISHES

Portugal is a small country; nevertheless its varied landscape and climate has led to many different local recipes, with each area growing its own crops and supporting different kinds of livestock. There are wonderful fish dishes from the coastal towns, and delicious soups and casseroles, made of meat, game, wild herbs and vegetables, from the inland villages. Local specialities are still made according to recipes handed down over many generations.

RIGHT Freshly baked Portuguese breads, tarts and pastries are popular in specialist bakeries around the world.

THE RURAL NORTH

The coastal area known as the Minho region in the north of Portugal stretches from the city of Porto up to the Spanish border. Each child traditionally inherits their own part of any property, and so smallholdings tend to be small indeed. Ingenuity is needed to grow food for the family, with vines strung high up over the top of vegetables to pack in the maximum yield from the land. Many families still keep a pig and a few chickens, which will be slaughtered in the autumn and made into cured meats for the winter, as well as *cachaço de porco* (braised pork) or a stew with vegetables, such as *coxa de frango com penca e grão* (chicken pieces with cabbage and chickpeas). Several kinds of corn, wheat and rye are grown, and many different

kinds of bread are made, the most popular being *broa*, made mainly with cornflour. The rivers of the Minho and Douro supply freshwater fish: shad and lamprey are a speciality, cooked with wine. Shad is prepared in thin slices and fried in olive oil till crispy, so its many thin scales almost disappear.

Further inland, where the Douro river flows through the mountains from Spain, is a wild landscape, with high peaks and deep gorges, and many vineyards, which cling precariously to the mountain slopes. This area is also renowned for game, and local hunters catch woodcock, partridge and hare, to be cooked in a low oven with wine and beans, and the wild mushrooms that grow in the forests. Partridge is traditionally stewed in the intense young ruby port, and wild mushrooms, such as ceps and trompetes, are simply mixed with scrambled eggs.

CENTRAL PORTUGAL

Travelling south from the Douro, we come to the Beiras, a large agricultural area in the centre of Portugal. There are great contrasts of temperature

RIGHT The deep Atlantic waters around Portugal's coast are abundant with marine life. Freshly caught fish, simply prepared, is a mainstay of the Portuguese diet.

in the inland area around Portugal's highest mountain, Serra da Estrela – cold in winter and hot in summer, it is a region of fierce tastes to match the extreme temperatures. The pork sausages are a speciality, particularly the *morcela* sausage, a blood pudding made with bread or rice, the blood of the slaughtered pig and lots of spicy cumin. Sometimes *morcela* will contain honey as well.

On the plains of Cova da Beira, below the mountains, all sorts of fruits are grown – cherries, figs, apples, pears and plums. These make wonderful desserts on their own or in the form of fruit tarts, fritters and sponge puddings. The goats of the central region give milk for a delightful, creamy and tasty *Serra* cheese, first made in this region and now loved by many Portuguese.

ON THE COAST

The sea around Portugal is rich in all sorts of fish and shellfish. Always fresh, the fish is grilled (broiled) or baked simply in the oven with slices of onion and tomato, and dressed with a good olive oil. The Portuguese also love fish stew, *caldeirada*, cooked slowly with lots of vegetable juices. Once again, pork dominates the meat recipes in the Bairrada area, with a whole roasted pig – *leitão* – cooked in an old-fashioned oven so that the meat becomes juicy and tender, and the outside is crispy and golden.

In the older parts of the capital, Lisbon, there are still a good number of *tasquinhas*, old-fashioned cafés, where you can have a glass of wine and various *petiscos* (lots of little dishes to taste): snails, bean salad, cod fishcakes and more. One curiosity is *peixinhos da horta* – green beans dipped in egg and flour – a dish which, legend has it, was taken to Japan by the Portuguese explorers and adopted by the Japanese as their *tempura*.

THE WARM SOUTH

South of the River Tagus, in the plains of the Alentejo, there are rolling fields of cork trees, wheat and vineyards. The land has traditionally been farmed in large estates, with poor workers doing wonders with their rich masters' leftovers, and the result is a creative cuisine, full of surprises. Wild asparagus, oregano and coriander (cilantro) are

added to filling bread soups, enriched with cheese or a tiny bit of meat. It's another hunting region, with many recipes for partridge, hare and grouse. The Alentejo is also the land of the black pig, made into wonderful cured ham and grilled pork dishes spiced with wild herbs.

At the foot of Portugal is the Algarve, where fig and almond trees are grown, ready to make fantastic desserts like *toucinho do ceu* (almond tart). This is where the *cataplana*, the traditional pressure-cooker cooking dish, was first used to steam fish and seafood to perfection.

THE ATLANTIC ISLANDS

Far out in the Atlantic lie the Portuguese islands of Madeira, Porto Santo and the Azores. Each of these has its own local delicacies, many of them based on fish from the surrounding deep waters. In Madeira, fish or meat is often accompanied by corn kernels combined with cornflour, then cut in slices and fried. In the Azores, fish or meat is stewed with grapes and saffron or cinnamon. Intriguingly, the inhabitants of the valley of Furnas in the Azores even use natural hot springs to cook their food by burying cooking pots in the sulphurous earth.

BELOW A group of cork strippers in Santana do Mato, near Coruche, sit down to lunch. Cork must be regularly harvested for some years before it is of a sufficient quality for use in wine bottles.

CLASSIC INGREDIENTS

The traditional Portuguese diet is very similar to that eaten in many Mediterranean countries. It is based on the simplest and tastiest of foods, such as bread, rice, olive oil, garlic, tomatoes and herbs. To these basic elements, the Portuguese cook will add small amounts of meat and fish – whatever is available (sometimes preserved) – and, most importantly, a variety of spices such as ground cumin, coriander and paprika, to make a strong-tasting, vibrant dish.

BELOW, CLOCKWISE FROM TOP LEFT
Black pudding (blood sausage) is made by cooking animal blood; *alheira* is a sausage that uses meats such as veal, duck and rabbit; *chouriço* is a spicy sausage made with pork and flavoured with pimentón (smoked paprika); and pork *bizaro* is a rich ham, produced by feeding pigs with chestnuts.

MEAT

Pork, lamb and poultry figure largely in Portuguese recipes, but were originally a treat available only to affluent landowners and noblemen. The exception was around the time of the slaughter of a family pig, of which every single part was eaten, including the pig's stomach (tripe) and blood (in *morcela*, blood sausage). Making sausage is a great way to preserve the meat for the cold winter months, and there are many variations, including *paio*, and *chouriço*, which involve marinating the meat and fat with garlic, bay leaves, paprika and salt. The sausage ingredients originally depended on what was grown locally and the imagination of the cook.

Poultry and lamb dishes are also common, usually cooked slowly with tomatoes or other vegetables and herbs, and bulked out with rice or potatoes. There's an interesting story that tells of the Jewish people of Portugal, forced to pretend to convert to Christianity during the 15th century, who devised a sausage made of chicken, veal and bread (*alheira*) so that they could look as if they were eating pork. This is still made today but now sometimes actually includes pork! Another tale explains why tripe is a favourite around the Porto area (in fact the people of Porto are often known as "tripe eaters" – *tripeiros*). Lisbon was blockaded by the Castilians in the 14th century and was running out of food. The selfless and heroic inhabitants of Porto, further up the coast, sent their own reserves of meat by sea to the besieged city and found themselves reduced to eating tripe instead of finer cuts of meat.

Beef is not a common dish in Portugal, but when it is eaten, it is usually in the form of a thin slice of steak quickly fried, which sometimes comes with an egg on top and is often accompanied by potatoes and olives.

The Portuguese are not discriminating about their meat recipes. In the past, if they had some meat to use, it was added to the pot; if not, they ate more vegetables and bulked them out with potatoes and rice. This gives rise to the wonderful *cozido a portuguesa*, a casserole dish containing as many different kinds of meat and vegetables as

you like, depending on what is to hand – maybe pork and pork sausage, lamb, ham, carrots, potatoes, rice, chickpeas and onions.

They also combine meat with seafood in a traditional dish of pork with clams – *porco com ameijoas* – a mixture of tastes and textures of which the Portuguese are very fond.

FISH AND SHELLFISH

Portugal has many great recipes for fish. Its livelihood and cultural history is bound up with the wild and relatively unpolluted Atlantic Ocean, which surrounds half the country. All kinds of fish and shellfish are eaten – sardines, prawns (shrimp), sea bass, swordfish, octopus, tuna, crab, mackerel, clams, oysters – mainly freshly grilled or baked in the oven with garlic, herbs and wine. Freshwater fish are popular too, such as lampreys and eel from several rivers in the north and centre of the country.

There are a couple of exceptions to the rule of putting fish straight from the sea on to the plate, however. One is *caldeirada*, a stew of any available fish or shellfish, which is simmered for a long time (and is therefore cooked mainly at weekends in the busy 21st century).

The other exception is *bacalhau*, salted cod, a staple ingredient of Portuguese cooking. The salting process arises from the time before freezer units, when fishermen made their way north over hundreds of miles of Atlantic seas to Newfoundland to fish for cod. To preserve the fish, the fishermen used to clean and gut them on board the boat, and kept adding layers of salt to the flattened cod until the hold was full. Only then would they turn for home, where the fish were dried in the sun.

Bacalhau has to be de-salted and hydrated before it can be cooked. It is divided into pieces – the best cuts are the fillets in the centre of the fish, and the end pieces will be used for stews and soups – and then soaked in several changes of fresh water over two days. Once most of the salt has been removed it is cooked and eaten straight away. You can buy de-salted *bacalhau* from supermarkets, ready to use, or to be kept in the freezer. Typical dishes combine the cod with potatoes, eggs, pancakes or bread for a substantial meal.

OLIVES AND OLIVE OIL

These ingredients are universally used. Each region has its own varieties of olives, and each village used to press its own olives in a *lagar*, a co-operative system which helped to give an efficient return on the harvest from each smallholding.

The northern region's olive oil is light, fresh and a brilliant green in colour; in the central Beiras, there is a flavour of almonds and dried fruit; in the hot southern region the olive oil is more mature and blends beautifully with cooked food.

Olive oil is used both in frying and grilling (broiling) fresh fish, and in marinating meat and fish for longer, slow cooking. It is also a major part of any salad dressing, of course, and can be eaten on its own just with a slice or two of bread. Olives, so plentiful in Portugal, are a key ingredient to many regional recipes, and are typically marinated with olive oil, oregano and slices of lemon.

ABOVE, CLOCKWISE FROM TOP LEFT
Bacalhau is a dry, salted cod that is an established feature of the Portuguese cuisine; prawns are fished around the mainland coastline and the two large island regions; the country is full of olive groves, and olives feature largely in the diet; and sardines total 40 per cent of Portugal's fresh fish production.

ABOVE, CLOCKWISE FROM TOP LEFT
Portuguese cheeses include the Queijo da Serra, a sheep cheese with a smooth consistency and delicate flavour, the creamy cheese of Azeitão and the sweet Serpa cheese from the Alentejo; turnip greens or turnip tops are slightly bitter tasting; wild mushrooms are used widely; and the locally grown tomatoes are the usual sweet-tasting Mediterranean treat.

DAIRY PRODUCE

The dairy industry in Portugal is based around cheese and butter rather than cow's milk. Northern Trás-os-Montes and Minho are renowned for their cheese and butter, and on the Azores their rich milk makes the cured Ilhas cheese. Cheese is rarely used for cooking. It is more often eaten on its own as part of an evening meal, or for lunch with a slice of bread.

The Portuguese make delicious creamy cheeses from goat's milk or sheep's milk. Serra da Estrela and Serpa cheese are favourites. These creamy, strongly flavoured cheeses can be eaten with a spoon – simply dig into a hole on the top – or cut into slices when more solid and mature.

Queijo fresco, a fresh, young cheese traditionally made with goat's milk, makes a light first course to a meal. The Portuguese eat it sprinkled with salt and accompanied by a tomato and oregano salad.

VEGETABLES

Many vegetables are grown in the accommodating climate, but the most universal are tomatoes and potatoes. Both of these were brought from the New World in the 15th and 16th centuries, and rapidly became the basis of all kinds of dishes, from salads to stews and soups to pies. *Bacalhau* (salt cod) has an affinity with potatoes and there are many recipes which use both with onions and garlic or olives. Another essential ingredient is the fiery chilli peppers (*piri piri*) that were brought to Portugal from Brazil, via Angola.

One of the most popular dishes in Portugal is *caldo verde*, the green cabbage soup made in the north. This is real solid peasant food, made with finely shredded *couve galega* (Galician cabbage), as well as a few chunks of sausage. It is usually eaten with crusty bread.

Vegetables add colour, flavour and, of course, nutritional value to many Portuguese dishes. The vivid green of broad (fava) beans, green beans, cabbage and asparagus is balanced in the stew by bright red tomatoes and (bell) peppers, and paler turnips, pumpkins, onions, garlic and potatoes.

DRIED BEANS, PEAS AND CHESTNUTS

Legumes (beans and peas) have always been dried as a part of any peasant cuisine, where families had to make the most of food that can be preserved for use in the colder months. Many Portuguese stews consist of large amounts of dried beans or chickpeas with small amounts of meat or fish – for example, the basic bean stew, *feijoada*, can be made of any kind of dried beans and vegetables, with or without meat. In the past, meat from the family pig could be braised slowly with chickpeas from the garden and wild mushrooms from the forest. Or if a hunter caught a hare, it could be combined with white haricot (navy) beans in a strong-tasting stew, *lebre com feijao*.

Wild chestnuts are used in savoury braised recipes, and are also eaten on their own in the autumn. Chestnuts are an acquired taste, and where once they would have been used for bulk, these days they are often replaced by potatoes or beans in a casserole.

HERBS AND SPICES

Some of the herbs and spices used so freely in Portuguese dishes are native to the country; others were imported. The spice trade began in earnest when the sea route to India was discovered in the late 15th century. Many exotic spices were adopted by Portuguese cooks and soon became integral to Portuguese cuisine, for example paprika, cumin, cinnamon, saffron, vanilla and black pepper.

Coriander (cilantro), oregano and parsley are perhaps the most commonly used herbs, lending their subtle flavour to meat, fish and vegetable dishes alike. They are also added to homemade sausages to give flavour to the meat. Thyme, rosemary, bay leaves, basil and tarragon are popular too in soups, casseroles, salad dressings and marinades.

BREAD AND RICE

The wheat, barley, rye and corn grown on the warm plains of central and southern Portugal are milled into flour for bread, cakes and desserts. There are many different varieties of flour, leading to interesting regional variations in bread recipes, even from one village to the next.

But bread is not only a base for cheese, a mopper-up of juices or a light breakfast. The Portuguese are very fond of adding bread to their soup to thicken it, and they also make *açordas*

and *migas*, mixtures of dried bread, stock, vegetables and egg in varying amounts – thinner for *açordas*; thicker and almost cake-like for *migas*.

Rice is not an indigenous crop, but has been so enthusiastically adopted that it figures in many recipes, both savoury and sweet. Most of these are quite moist, with plenty of juices. You can find rice in soups, in stews of meat or fish, as the basis of a risotto-like *arroz de marisco* (seafood rice) or just with honey or sugar and topped with cinnamon in the Portuguese version of rice pudding, *arroz doce*.

FRUIT, NUTS AND SWEET THINGS

Citrus fruits were brought to the country by the Moors in the 8th century, along with almonds and figs, and these all flourish in the hot summers and warm winters of the Algarve and the Douro region. Fruits and almonds are often combined with honey and sponge cake, eggs or pastry to make a substantial dessert.

There is a delightful tradition, which started in the 17th century, when the nuns in the Azores baked cakes and pastries to raise funds for their convent. The names given to these tasty morsels reveal quite a sense of humour among the sisters – *papos de anjo* (angels' cheeks) and *barrigas de freiras* (nuns' bellies), to name but two – and they are very sweet confections of flour, egg and sugar.

PETISCOS & APPETIZERS

Indulge in a tasty snack, or get your meal started with a small dish of something tempting – a refreshing salad, crunchy deep-fried vegetables, or a seafood appetizer, maybe accompanied by a glass of Portuguese wine.

THE PORTUGUESE, like other Mediterranean people, enjoy gathering round the table to eat, drink and talk, and *petiscos* are the ideal food for this kind of occasion. A sunny afternoon in the countryside with the family, meeting friends before going home from work, doing a business deal – these are all perfect excuses to enjoy *petiscos* and a glass of wine.

A *petisco* is a small dish of something tasty to awaken the appetite, served with a drink. It's not like an appetizer, which usually consists of just one dish before you move on to the main course – in a restaurant you are more likely to be presented with a whole range of *petiscos* to share with your friends so that you can try the different flavours and textures. These dishes can be as simple as a little plateful of grilled (broiled) sausage, smoked or salted hams, different types of cheese sliced very thinly, some dark bread and dried fruits. But there are a lot more to try, such as deep-fried morsels of squid or octopus in batter, little fish croquettes, or vegetable pastries. Sample a few of these delicious nibbles with pieces of fine quality bread, have a glass of wine and enjoy the company!

Your appetizer before the main course may be a more solid plateful of a single vegetable, some marinated fish or a simple salad. Fish and shellfish are very popular, for example *salada de polvo* (octopus salad) or *sardinhas de escabeche* (sardines in tomato and onion marinade). You might be tempted to try the local soup recipe, but unless you've got a huge appetite from a day swimming in the sea or walking in the hills, make sure it's not one of the filling bread or bean soups so popular in Portugal, which would make a meal in itself. Now is your chance to sample mushrooms marinated in a local wine and olive oil (*cogumelos marinados*), or the green beans deep-fried in a light batter (*peixinhos da horta*). Stronger flavours can be found in a dish of warm figs with ham and a port wine sauce, or a stuffed spider crab (*santola recheada*). And if you're very hungry, there are several traditional appetizers that include beans or chickpeas with a small piece of fish and salad, blending the bland flavour of the beans with a piquant dressing and the saltiness of the seafood.

TOMATO SALAD WITH MARINATED PEPPERS AND OREGANO

TOMATE COM PIMENTOS MARINADOS E OREGÃOS

The Portuguese usually prepare this refreshing appetizer with home-grown tomatoes for maximum flavour and sweetness. They combine superbly with marinated peppers, which, because they have been well roasted before soaking, are sweeter and more digestible than raw ones.

1 If the marinated peppers are in large pieces, cut them into strips. Arrange the tomato slices and pepper strips on a serving dish, sprinkle with the oregano and season to taste with sea salt.

2 Whisk together the olive oil and vinegar in a jug (pitcher) and pour the dressing over the salad. Serve immediately or cover and chill in the refrigerator until required.

SERVES 4–6

2 marinated (bell) peppers, drained
6 ripe tomatoes, sliced
15ml/1 tbsp chopped fresh oregano
75ml/5 tbsp olive oil
30ml/2 tbsp white wine vinegar
sea salt

COOK'S TIPS

• Marinated (bell) peppers are widely available in jars, often labelled as pimentos. However, they are much tastier when prepared yourself. To do this, wrap one green and one red pepper in foil and place on a baking sheet. Cook in a preheated oven at 180°C/350°F/Gas 4, or under a preheated grill (broiler), turning occasionally, for 20–30 minutes, until tender. Unwrap and when cool, peel the peppers, then halve and seed. Cut the flesh into strips and pack into a screw-top jar. Add olive oil to cover, close and store in the refrigerator for up to 6 days.

• You can preserve marinated peppers by cooking them in a closed jar in boiling water for about 30 minutes. They can then be kept for approximately 6 weeks.

PER PORTION Energy 119kcal/494kJ; Protein 1.4g; Carbohydrate 6.9g, of which sugars 6.7g; Fat 9.7g, of which saturates 1.5g; Cholesterol 0mg; Calcium 17mg; Fibre 2.1g; Sodium 12mg.

SERVES 4

400g/14oz mixed mushrooms, such as chestnut and oyster mushrooms

30ml/2 tbsp olive oil

200g/7oz raw ham, sausages and bacon, diced

2 garlic cloves, finely chopped

15–30ml/1–2 tbsp white wine vinegar

45ml/3 tbsp chopped fresh parsley

VARIATION

When served hot, these mushrooms also go well with scrambled eggs.

PER PORTION Energy 130kcal/541kJ; Protein 12.1g; Carbohydrate 3.1g, of which sugars 1g; Fat 7.8g, of which saturates 1.5g; Cholesterol 29mg; Calcium 20mg; Fibre 1.8g; Sodium 607mg.

MARINATED MUSHROOMS

COGUMELOS MARINADOS

This dish is usually served cold but tastes equally good hot from the pan. Use as many varieties of mushrooms as you like to make the most of their various flavours and textures. This is a resourceful way of using up a solitary sausage or a couple of slices of bacon or ham.

1 Wipe the mushrooms clean and cut or tear the larger ones in half or quarters.

2 Heat the olive oil in a frying pan. Add the meat and cook over a low heat, stirring frequently, for about 5 minutes.

3 Add the mushrooms, increase the heat to high and cook, stirring constantly, for 5 minutes. Add the garlic and 15ml/1 tbsp of the vinegar and cook for 1 minute more.

4 Remove the pan from the heat and stir in the parsley. Serve immediately or, if you want to serve the mushrooms cold, add the remaining vinegar and leave to cool.

SERVES 4

400g/14oz green beans
100g/3¾oz/scant 1 cup plain
(all-purpose) flour
1 egg
vegetable oil, for deep-frying
salt

VARIATION

While not traditionally Portuguese, you can prepare other vegetables in the same way. Try mushrooms, red (bell) pepper strips or carrots cut into thin batons.

GREEN BEANS TEMPURA

PEIXINHOS DA HORTA

A literal translation of *peixinhos da horta* is "from the field where you plant vegetables". The dish is distinguished by the green beans, which are coated in a light tempura batter. This cooking technique is thought to have been taken to Japan by Portuguese sailors in the early days of exploration.

1 Trim the beans and blanch them in a large pan of boiling water for 1 minute. Drain and refresh in iced water, then drain again well.

2 Sift the flour into a bowl and stir in enough cold water to make a medium paste. Add the egg and beat well, then season with salt.

3 Heat the oil in a large pan or deep-fryer to 170°C/340°F or until a cube of day-old bread browns in 40 seconds. Dip the beans in the batter to coat, add to the hot oil and deep-fry until crisp and golden brown. Drain on kitchen paper and serve immediately.

PER PORTION Energy 227kcal/945kJ; Protein 5.8g; Carbohydrate 22.6g, of which sugars 2.7g; Fat 13.2g, of which saturates 1.8g; Cholesterol 48mg; Calcium 78mg; Fibre 3g; Sodium 18mg.

BROAD BEANS WITH SAUSAGES
FAVAS COM ENCHIDOS

When broad beans are in season, they are said to "jump" from the field into the pot, and this dish is undoubtedly a bean-lover's dream. Nowadays, you can prepare it throughout the year, as beans don't lose much quality when they are frozen. Nevertheless, extremely tender young beans are best and will need only a little cooking, especially if you have the patience to pop them from their skins first.

1 Heat the olive oil in a pan. Add the onion and cook over a low heat, stirring occasionally, for about 5 minutes, until softened.

2 Meanwhile, cut the black pudding and sausage into small pieces. Add them to the pan with the bacon and garlic and simmer gently, stirring occasionally, for 20 minutes.

3 Pop the beans out of their skins and add to the pan with the paprika. Stir, then pour in enough stock to cover and simmer until the beans are just tender. Garnish with chopped coriander.

SERVES 4

30ml/2 tbsp olive oil
1 onion, chopped
150g/5oz black pudding (blood sausage)
150g/5oz *chouriço* sausage
50g/2oz /⅓ cup diced bacon
1 garlic clove, chopped
400g/14oz shelled broad (fava) beans
15ml/1 tbsp paprika
150–300ml/¼–½ pint/⅔–1¼ cups chicken stock
chopped fresh coriander (cilantro), to garnish

COOK'S TIPS

• You can serve this as a main dish with poached eggs and crusty bread.
• As a variation, cut 150g/5oz black pudding (blood sausage) in 1.5cm/⅔in slices and grill (broil) or fry, then add to the ready cooked beans.

PER PORTION Energy 286kcal/1191kJ; Protein 15.1g; Carbohydrate 16.7g, of which sugars 2.4g; Fat 18.1g, of which saturates 5.2g; Cholesterol 29mg; Calcium 103mg; Fibre 6.9g; Sodium 626mg.

SMALL CHICKEN PIES
EMPADA DE GALINHA

These little pies can be filled with different kinds of meat – although chicken is the most popular, they are also good with a mixture of game and chicken, or with fish or shellfish. They make a tempting afternoon snack or you could have two or three of them with a refreshing salad for a delicious light lunch.

MAKES ABOUT 12

1 chicken, weighing 1.6–2kg/3½–4½ lb
45ml/3 tbsp olive oil
1 sausage, weighing about 250g/9oz
150g/5oz bacon
1 garlic clove
10 black peppercorns
1 onion stuck with 2 cloves
1 bunch of parsley, chopped
4 thyme or marjoram sprigs
juice of 1 lemon or 60ml/4 tbsp white wine vinegar
butter, for greasing
500g/1¼ lb puff pastry, thawed if frozen
plain (all-purpose) flour, for dusting
2 egg yolks, lightly beaten
salt

1 Cut the chicken into pieces. Heat the oil in a large, heavy pan. Add the chicken pieces and cook over a medium-low heat, turning occasionally, for about 10 minutes, until golden brown on all sides.

2 Now add the sausage, bacon, garlic, peppercorns, onion, parsley, thyme and lemon juice or vinegar. Pour in enough water to cover and bring to the boil. Lower the heat, cover and simmer for 1–1½ hours, until tender.

3 Remove all the meat from the stock with a slotted spoon. Then return the stock to the heat and cook, uncovered, until slightly reduced. Strain the stock into a bowl and season with salt to taste.

4 Remove and discard the chicken skin and bones and cut the meat into small pieces. Cut the sausage and bacon into small pieces. Mix all the meat together. Preheat the oven to 200°C/400°F/Gas 6. Grease a 12-cup muffin tin (pan) with butter.

VARIATION

You can use the following dough as an alternative to puff pastry. Sift 500g/1¼ lb/5 cups plain (all-purpose) flour into a bowl and make a well in the centre. Add 5 eggs and about 150g/5oz/⅔ cup of the leftover chicken fat to the well and mix together, adding some stock if necessary. Blend well, then shape into a ball and leave to rest for 30 minutes before rolling out.

5 Roll out the pastry thinly on a lightly floured surface and stamp out 12 rounds with a 7.5cm/3in cutter. Gather the trimmings together and roll out thinly again, then stamp out 12 rounds with a 6cm/2½in cutter.

6 Place the larger rounds in the cups of the prepared tin, pressing the pastry to the side with your thumb, and divide the meat among them. Spoon in a little of the stock, then brush the edges with beaten egg yolk and cover with the smaller rounds, pinching the edges to seal. Brush the remaining egg yolk over the top to glaze and make a small hole in the centre of each pie with a wooden cocktail stick (toothpick).

7 Bake for 15–25 minutes, until golden brown. Remove from the oven and leave to cool before serving.

PER PIE Energy 368kcal/1534kJ; Protein 24.5g; Carbohydrate 18.3g, of which sugars 1.2g; Fat 22.8g, of which saturates 4.3g; Cholesterol 109mg; Calcium 44mg; Fibre 0.2g; Sodium 547mg.

SCRAMBLED EGGS WITH *CHOURIÇO* AND GREEN ASPARAGUS

OVOS MEXIDOS COM ENCHIDOS E ESPARGOS VERDES

Egg dishes are very popular in Portugal. Poached eggs are served with broad beans, peas or in a tomato soup; omelettes are filled with goat's cheese or salt cod; eggs are fried with ham or onion; and last but not least, eggs are scrambled with wild mushrooms, tomatoes and different kind of sausages. This dish is particularly tempting. It works best with wild asparagus.

1 Trim off any woody ends from the asparagus and wash thoroughly. Tie the spears together and place them upright in a tall pan of salted boiling water. Alternatively, you can cook them lying flat in a frying pan filled with salted boiling water. Depending on the thickness, cook for 10–20 minutes, until tender. Drain well and refresh in iced water. Drain again and cut into small pieces.

2 Heat the olive oil in a large frying pan. Add the bacon and sausage and cook over a low heat, stirring occasionally, for 8–10 minutes, until lightly browned and cooked through.

3 Add the eggs, croûtons and asparagus and cook, stirring frequently, until the eggs are just set. Serve immediately.

SERVES 4

1 bunch of green asparagus

100ml/3½ fl oz/scant ½ cup olive oil

100g/3¾ oz bacon, diced

1 *chouriço* sausage, weighing about 100g/3¾ oz, diced

8 eggs, beaten

100g/3¾ oz bread croûtons

PER PORTION Energy 550kcal/2283kJ; Protein 25g; Carbohydrate 16.5g, of which sugars 2.3g; Fat 43.4g, of which saturates 10.8g; Cholesterol 410mg; Calcium 115mg; Fibre 1.6g; Sodium 1051mg.

SERVES 6

1 tomato

250g/9oz salt cod, soaked

500g/1¼ lb canned chickpeas, drained and rinsed

1 small onion, chopped

1 small bunch of coriander (cilantro), chopped

75–105ml/5–7 tbsp olive oil

30–45 ml/2–3 tbsp white wine vinegar

VARIATION

You can also make this salad with cubes of raw tuna loin fillet. Cut 350g/12oz of fresh tuna into cubes and marinate in some red wine vinegar with a good twist of black pepper and a little Worcestershire sauce for half hour, and combine it with the other ingredients.

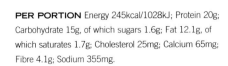

PER PORTION Energy 245kcal/1028kJ; Protein 20g; Carbohydrate 15g, of which sugars 1.6g; Fat 12.1g, of which saturates 1.7g; Cholesterol 25mg; Calcium 65mg; Fibre 4.1g; Sodium 355mg.

CODFISH WITH CHICKPEAS
BACALHAU COM GRÃO

Fresh coriander is used in many dishes in southern Portugal. In this region, salt cod is often served almost raw, although thoroughly soaked to remove the salt, and accompanied only with some olive oil and vinegar. However, in this recipe, you can cook the fish to your taste first.

1 Cut the tomato into quarters, scoop out the seeds and dice the flesh. Place the cod in boiling water and let it stand away from the heat for 5 minutes. Then drain the water and slice the fish (cleaned of skin and bones).

2 Put the cod, chickpeas, onion and coriander in a serving dish and mix gently. Add olive oil and vinegar to taste and toss lightly. Sprinkle the salad with the diced tomato.

STUFFED HORSE MACKEREL
CARAPAU RECHEADO

Horse mackerel, also known as scad, is a member of the widespread fish family that also includes jacks, pompanos, trevallys, kingfish and queenfish. Their bony platelets make them look unattractive and they are often only used as bait, although once the platelets are removed, they make good eating. This recipe originated in the *Açores* (Portuguese Azores) and was prepared by very poor people. Nevertheless it is a first-rate, delicious dish, using a highly underrated fish.

1 Cut off and discard the fish heads. To scale them, hold each fish by the tail and scrape off the scales with a fish scaler or serrated knife held at an angle, working from head to tail. Rinse well under cold running water. Open out the fish, skin side uppermost – you may need to extend the slit in the bellies. Press along the backbones with your thumb. Turn the fish over and ease out the bones. Remove any remaining bones with a sharp knife, your finger or tweezers.

2 Heat the olive oil in a frying pan. Add the onion and green pepper and cook over a low heat, stirring occasionally, for 5 minutes, until softened. Add the garlic, paprika paste and tomato and cook for a few minutes more, then remove the pan from the heat.

3 Tear the bread into pieces and mash to a paste with water. Stir the paste into the pan and season to taste with salt and vinegar. Stir in the parsley and olives.

4 Heat the oil for deep-frying to 180°C/350°F or until a cube of day-old bread browns in 40 seconds. Meanwhile, divide the filling among four of the fish. Place the remaining fish on top and secure with wooden cocktail sticks (toothpicks). Dust each pair of fish with cornflour, shaking off any excess, add to the hot oil and deep-fry for about 5 minutes, until golden brown and cooked through. Drain on kitchen paper and serve immediately.

SERVES 4

8 small horse mackerel, about 10cm/4in long, gutted
30ml/2 tbsp olive oil
1 small onion, chopped
1 green (bell) pepper, seeded and cut in small cubes
1 garlic clove, chopped
15ml/1 tbsp paprika paste
1 tomato, peeled and diced
2 slices day-old bread, crusts removed
5–10ml/1–2 tsp white wine vinegar
30ml/2 tbsp chopped fresh parsley
25g/1oz/¼ cup pitted green olives, cut into small strips
cornflour (cornstarch), for dusting
vegetable oil, for deep-frying
salt

VARIATION

Serve with whole new potatoes, gently roasted in olive oil until golden and soft-centred, for an excellent main course.

PER PORTION Energy 558kcal/2316kJ; Protein 30.4g; Carbohydrate 15.2g, of which sugars 4.9g; Fat 42.1g, of which saturates 7.2g; Cholesterol 81mg; Calcium 70mg; Fibre 2.2g; Sodium 316mg.

SERVES 6

1 bunch of parsley

1 bay leaf

2 garlic cloves

75ml/5 tbsp white wine vinegar

600g/1lb 6oz fresh hard roe

75ml/5 tbsp olive oil

2 marinated (bell) peppers, drained

sea salt

VARIATIONS

• To serve fresh roe as a main course, place it in an ovenproof dish, drizzle generously with olive oil and sprinkle with salt. Bake in a preheated oven at 180°C/350°F/Gas 4 for 10–15 minutes. Serve with cabbage and potatoes.

• Another option is to mash the fish roe with a little olive oil and then use the paste to make simple, yet delicious, canapes. Serve decorated with the marinated bell peppers.

PER PORTION Energy 207kcal/862kJ; Protein 22.4g; Carbohydrate 3.9g, of which sugars 3.7g; Fat 11.4g, of which saturates 1.8g; Cholesterol 330mg; Calcium 24mg; Fibre 1.1g; Sodium 114mg.

FISH ROE WITH MARINATED PEPPERS

OVAS DE PEIXE COM PIMENTOS MARINADOS

Originally a leftover ingredient, fresh fish roe is now considered to be a real delicacy in Portugal, along with some other southern European countries, although it has rather gone out of favour elsewhere. Despite this, smoked and preserved roe are still widely available. This cheap ingredient is a Portuguese favourite that is used in a number of traditional dishes. For this recipe, you will require fresh hard roe, preferably from hake or cod.

1 Chop the most tender parsley leaves and reserve the stalks and any remaining leaves.

2 Place the reserved parsley leaves and stalks, the bay leaf, garlic, 15ml/1 tbsp of the vinegar and a pinch of sea salt in a large, shallow pan.

3 Add the roe to the pan, and enough water to cover. Bring just to the boil, then lower the heat until the water is barely simmering. Gently poach the roe for 10–15 minutes, until firm. Remove with a slotted spatula and leave to cool.

4 Whisk together the olive oil, the remaining vinegar and the chopped parsley in a bowl. Cut the marinated peppers into strips, if necessary, and then cut the roe into 1cm/½in slices.

5 Add the pepper strips and slices of roe to the vinaigrette and toss gently. Transfer to individual plates and serve immediately.

SERVES 6

1 apple

240g/8½oz canned tuna, drained

500g/1¼lb canned black-eyed beans
(peas), drained and rinsed

1 small onion, chopped

30ml/2 tbsp chopped fresh parsley

75–105ml/5–7 tbsp olive oil

30–45ml/2–3 tbsp white wine vinegar

VARIATION

This salad can also be served as a main
dish. In this case, substitute cooked,
diced potatoes for the apple, and sprinkle
with chopped hard-boiled egg to cover.
Heat gently in a pan before serving.

PER PORTION Energy 139kcal/588kJ; Protein 15.4g;
Carbohydrate 16.7g, of which sugars 4.6g; Fat 1.6g, of
which saturates 0.3g; Cholesterol 20mg; Calcium 70mg;
Fibre 5.6g; Sodium 454mg.

TUNA SALAD WITH BLACK-EYED BEANS

ATUM COM FEIJÃO FRADE

Very simple and easy to prepare, this salad is deliciously fresh tasting. It is
popular with both adults and children and is a useful stand-by when
unexpected guests arrive. It even works well for picnics.

1 Peel, quarter and core the apple, then slice thinly. Put the apple, tuna, beans, onion
and parsley in a salad bowl and mix gently.

2 Whisk together the olive oil and vinegar to taste in a bowl, then pour over the salad.
Toss gently to coat.

SERVES 4-6

12 sardines, cleaned

plain (all-purpose) flour, for dusting

150ml/¼ pint/⅔ cup olive oil

2 onions, halved and thinly sliced

3 bay leaves

2 garlic cloves, chopped

150ml/¼ pint/⅔ cup white wine vinegar

2 ripe tomatoes, diced

sea salt

crusty bread, to serve

COOK'S TIP

Leave the sardine marinade for some days and don't be shy with the vinegar, as it will be absorbed.

PER PORTION Energy 335kcal/1392kJ; Protein 21.2g; Carbohydrate 4.3g, of which sugars 1.1g; Fat 26g, of which saturates 5.1g; Cholesterol 0mg; Calcium 92mg; Fibre 0.5g; Sodium 123mg.

SARDINES IN ONION AND TOMATO MARINADE

SARDINHAS DE ESCABECHE

Both fish and poultry are frequently marinated in Portuguese cooking. The basic marinade consists of onion, garlic, bay leaves and good-quality wine vinegar, to which tomatoes or other vegetables may be added. The sardines that are fished off Portugal's cold Atlantic coast are particularly fine.

1 Dust the sardines with flour, shaking off any excess. Heat 75ml/5 tbsp of the olive oil in a heavy frying pan. Add the sardines, in batches, and cook over a medium heat, for about 1 minute each side. Remove with a slotted spatula and drain on kitchen paper.

2 In a clean pan, cook the onions, bay leaves and garlic with the rest of the olive oil over a low heat, stirring occasionally, for about 5 minutes, until softened. Add the vinegar and the tomatoes, and season with sea salt to taste.

3 Return the sardines to the pan. If they are not completely covered, add a little water or some more vinegar. Cook for a few minutes. Transfer the mixture to a deep plate, allow to cool and leave to marinate in the refrigerator for 3 days. Serve with crusty bread.

SARDINE "CUTLETS"

COSTELETAS DE SARDINHA

The most popular way to cook sardines is simply to grill them. They are usually served with tomato salad, potatoes and olive oil, but if you are at an informal barbecue, you can eat them on a slice of bread. Place the grilled sardine on the bread and nibble away at the fish until only the bones and head remain. Repeat this once or twice and then enjoy the bread soaked with the cooking juices. The cutlets featured here are a more sophisticated way of enjoying them.

1 To scale the sardines, hold each fish by the tail and scrape off the scales with a fish scaler or serrated knife held at an angle, working from head to tail. Rinse well under cold running water. Slit open the belly of each fish with a sharp knife or kitchen scissors and pull out the intestines with your fingers. Rinse well again. Open out the fish, skin side uppermost, and press along the backbone with your thumb. Turn the fish over and ease out the bones.

2 Place the sardines in a non-metallic dish and pour the lemon juice over them. Sprinkle them with salt and garlic, if using. Leave to marinate for 30 minutes.

3 Beat the eggs in a shallow dish. Spread out the flour in another shallow dish and spread out the breadcrumbs in a third. Heat the oil in a large pan or deep-fryer to 180°C/350°F or until a cube of day-old bread browns in 40 seconds.

4 Meanwhile, dip the sardines in the flour to coat, shaking off any excess, then dip them in the beaten egg and, finally, in the breadcrumbs. Add them to the hot oil, in batches if necessary, and deep-fry for 5 minutes, until golden brown and cooked through. Drain on kitchen paper and serve immediately.

SERVES 4

12 medium sardines
juice of 2 lemons
1 garlic clove, finely chopped (optional)
3 eggs
50g/2oz/½ cup plain (all-purpose) flour
50g/2oz/1 cup breadcrumbs
vegetable oil, for deep-frying
salt

COOK'S TIPS

• These sardines go particularly well with Green Beans Tempura (see page 26).

• For a cleaner dinner table, remove the sardine heads, along with the backbones, at the end of step 1.

PER PORTION Energy 489kcal/2042kJ; Protein 38.2g; Carbohydrate 19.4g, of which sugars 0.5g; Fat 29.4g, of which saturates 6.5g; Cholesterol 143mg; Calcium 181mg; Fibre 0.7g; Sodium 328mg.

OCTOPUS SALAD

SALADA DE POLVO

Octopus is a popular appetizer and is often served at Christmas. Served cold with plenty of parsley, as here, the octopus flavour is less intense. This will serve eight people as a small snack or four for a more substantial appetizer.

1 Rinse the octopus in plenty of water and cut off the body. Turn the body inside out and pull out and discard the entrails. Remove the little strips from the sides of the body. Rinse thoroughly again and turn the right way out. Squeeze out the beak. Beat the tentacles lightly with a rolling pin or the flat side of a meat mallet.

2 Half fill a large pan with water and add all the ingredients for the stock. Bring to the boil, then lower the heat and simmer for 10 minutes.

3 Add the octopus and bring back to the boil. Lower the heat slightly so that the liquid continues to boil and cook for 1 hour. Check with a fork to see if the octopus is tender. If not, cook for a little longer but check frequently because it will toughen if overcooked. Strain the stock into a bowl and reserve. Discard the flavourings.

4 Whisk together the olive oil and vinegar in a bowl, then stir in the onion and parsley. Taste and add more vinegar if you like an acidic vinaigrette.

5 Cut the octopus tentacles into 2cm/¾in pieces and place in a dish. Pour the vinaigrette over them and leave to stand for several hours before serving.

SERVES 4–8

1 uncooked octopus, weighing 2–3kg/4½–6½ lb
105ml/7 tbsp olive oil
30–45ml/2–3 tbsp white wine vinegar
1 onion, finely chopped
1 bunch of parsley, chopped

For the stock

2 onions, quartered
1 leek, chopped
3 garlic cloves, crushed
10 black peppercorns
2 bay leaves
pinch of salt

COOK'S TIPS

• You can buy octopus ready prepared, in which case miss out steps 1–3. If you need to cook a ready prepared octopus, check that it has been tenderized.
• An alternative way of tenderizing the tentacles is to seal them in a plastic bag and place in the freezer for 2 weeks. Thaw for 24 hours in the refrigerator before cooking.
• Reserve the octopus body to make Braised Octopus with Rice (see page 80).

PER PORTION Energy 199kcal/834kJ; Protein 30g; Carbohydrate 0.5g, of which sugars 0.3g; Fat 8.6g, of which saturates 1.4g; Cholesterol 80mg; Calcium 60mg; Fibre 0.2g; Sodium 1mg.

SERVES 4

600g/1lb 6oz live clams

100ml/3½fl oz/scant ½ cup olive oil

2 garlic cloves, very finely chopped

1 lemon

1 bunch of fresh coriander (cilantro), chopped

COOK'S TIP

All shellfish deteriorates very rapidly once out of the sea. Buy clams from a reputable supplier and cook them on the day of purchase. It is unwise to collect clams from the beach because of the risk of pollution.

PER PORTION Energy 197kcal/816kJ; Protein 8.9g; Carbohydrate 2.3g, of which sugars 0.4g; Fat 17g, of which saturates 2.5g; Cholesterol 34mg; Calcium 63mg; Fibre 0.9g; Sodium 605mg.

CLAMS WITH FRESH CORIANDER
AMÊIJOAS À BULHÃO PATO

This is the most common way to prepare clams in Portugal and also one of the most effective ways to enjoy their flavour. The smaller black-shelled clams found along Portugal's Atlantic coast are ideal, but there are many excellent types to be found all over the world. For a more substantial main dish, add butter beans and mashed tomato and serve with crusty bread.

1 Scrub the clams under cold running water. Discard any with broken shells or that do not shut immediately when sharply tapped.

2 Heat the olive oil in a large, heavy pan. Add the clams and garlic, cover with a tight-fitting lid and cook, shaking the pan frequently, for 3–5 minutes, until the shells open. Discard any that remain closed.

3 Halve the lemon and then squeeze the juice from one half into a bowl. Cut the other lemon half into wedges. Add the coriander and lemon juice to the clams and serve immediately with the lemon wedges.

SERVES 2–3

1 bay leaf

6 black peppercorns

1 onion

4 fresh parsley sprigs

500ml/17fl oz/generous 2 cups white wine

1 live spider crab, weighing about 1kg/2¼ lb

1 egg yolk

175ml/6fl oz/¾ cup olive oil

15ml/1 tbsp pickles, drained and chopped

5ml/1 tsp Worchester sauce

few drops of Tabasco sauce

5ml/1 tsp brandy

1 hard-boiled egg, chopped

sea salt

COOK'S TIP

Many people believe that placing a live crab in the freezer for 2–3 hours induces hypothermia and is a more humane way to kill it. Those who would rather avoid this stage altogether can buy a freshly cooked crab and omit step 1.

PER PORTION Energy 507kcal/2093kJ; Protein 16.4g; Carbohydrate 0.3g, of which sugars 0.2g; Fat 48.6g, of which saturates 7.3g; Cholesterol 167mg; Calcium 40mg; Fibre 0g; Sodium 290mg.

STUFFED SPIDER CRAB
SANTOLA RECHEADA

Widely found throughout Portugal, stuffed spider crab is the perfect dish to accompany a chilled beer on a sunny afternoon. With its very long legs, oval body and spiny shell, the crab's resemblance to a spider is quite remarkable. It has very sweet and succulent flesh. You can also prepare other kinds of crab in the same way.

1 Fill a large pan with water, measuring the quantity as you pour it in. Add the bay leaf, peppercorns, onion, parsley, white wine and 15ml/1 tbsp sea salt for every 1 litre/ 1¾ pints/4 cups water. Bring to the boil, add the crab, cover tightly and cook about 40 minutes. (Allow 20 minutes per 500g/1¼ lb crab.)

2 Remove the crab from the pan and leave until cool enough to handle. Break off the claws and legs. Turn the crab upside down and break off the tail flap. Insert a sturdy knife between the body and the back shell and twist it. Using your thumbs, press the body away from the shell. Remove and discard the gills.

3 Scoop out the brown meat into a bowl. Cut the body in half and scoop out all the white meat into another bowl. Crack the claws with the back of a heavy knife and pick out the white meat.

4 Place the back shell on a board and press down on the piece of shell just behind the eyes. When it snaps, remove and discard it, including the stomach. Scoop the remaining brown meat into the first bowl. Scrub the back shell, dry with kitchen paper and reserve.

5 Add the egg yolk to the bowl of brown meat and blend with a whisk. Gradually add the olive oil, a few drops at a time, whisking constantly. When about half of it has been incorporated, add it in a steady trickle, whisking constantly, until the mixture has the consistency of mayonnaise.

6 Fold in the white meat and pickles and stir in the Worcestershire sauce, Tabasco and brandy. Pile the mixture into the reserved shell and sprinkle with the hard-boiled egg. Serve with the legs to break at the table.

SOUPS

Whether you are seeking a light broth as an appetizer or a substantial soup for a main course, this selection will provide a variety of delicious and warming options.

SOUPS PLAY AN IMPORTANT ROLE in the Portuguese diet. Whether we are talking about a really bulky affair containing bread, vegetables and fish or sausage, or a lighter *tomatada* (made of fresh tomatoes), soup is a favourite dish. It is quite common to have soup as the first course to a meal – the Portuguese say it will "line the stomach". However, the soup can also be extremely filling, as it was originally made to satisfy the appetite and nutritional needs of farm workers after a hard day's work in the fields, or of fishermen after a night battling with the Atlantic for a catch of shrimp or sardines. It is the addition of bread or rice that really makes the difference between a light appetizer and a whole meal in a bowl.

One of Portugal's most popular soups is *caldo verde*, from the north of the country. It is prepared with a particular type of cabbage – Portuguese (or Galician) cabbage – that is a very bright green colour and grows 1m/1yd tall. The cabbage leaves are sliced very thinly and added to a simmering broth of potatoes and onion, with a whole sausage added for flavour. *Caldo verde* is served in a bowl with pieces of the same sausage and a dash of olive oil. Slices of corn bread are the perfect accompaniment.

There is a legend in Portugal about a soup called *sopa da pedra*, literally "stone soup". A poor traveller made a soup with nothing more than hot water and a stone in a borrowed pot. The townspeople felt sorry for this poor man, and one after another they came to add a vegetable, some seasoning, some bread and a sliced sausage until he had a good nourishing broth, which he ate with gusto. *Sopa da pedra* (containing no stones) is still served in the town of Almeirim in the Ribatejo area, north of Lisbon, where this traveller is said to have made the first-ever stone soup.

A Portuguese soup differs from a stew because of the texture of the dish. Although the ingredients may be remarkably similar, a stew will be thicker, maybe with larger chunks of meat, fish and vegetables; soup uses the less prime cuts of meat and fish (pigs' trotters or head meat; tail-ends and heads of fish) with finely chopped vegetables, sometimes pressed through a sieve (strainer) for a fine, smooth broth.

SERVES 4

500g/1¼ lb floury potatoes, cut into pieces

2 onions, chopped

300g/11oz Savoy cabbage

300g/11oz green beans, cut into 1cm/½in lengths

1 small bunch of fresh summer savory, chopped

50ml/2fl oz/¼ cup olive oil

salt

PER PORTION Energy 239kcal/998kJ; Protein 6.2g; Carbohydrate 34.2g, of which sugars 11.7g; Fat 9.6g, of which saturates 1.4g; Cholesterol 0mg; Calcium 96mg; Fibre 6.1g; Sodium 20mg.

GREEN BEAN AND CABBAGE SOUP

SOPA DE FEIJÃO VERDE COM SEGURELHA

This soup is found all over Portugal, but it is most popular in the central Ribatejo region. Here, the locals consider the addition of summer savory as essential to the recipe's success, and this aromatic, pungent herb does have a natural affinity with all kinds of beans.

1 Put the potatoes and onions in a large pan, add 1 litre/1¾ pints/4 cups water and bring to the boil. Cover and simmer for about 20 minutes, until tender.

2 Transfer the vegetables and cooking liquid to a food processor or blender and process to a purée. Return to the rinsed-out pan.

3 Cut the cabbage in quarters, cut out the core and slice in 2.5cm/1in pieces. Add the cabbage, the beans and summer savory to the pan and cook over a medium heat for a few minutes, until the cabbage is cooked, and the beans are tender but still slightly crisp.

4 Season with salt to taste, stir in the olive oil and serve immediately.

CHESTNUT AND WHITE BEAN SOUP
SOPA DE CASTANHAS E FEIJÃO BRANCO

In the northern Minho, this soup was once prepared during Lent, the weeks leading up to Easter during which Christians were forbidden to eat meat. It is quite substantial and was a good way of supplying energy to the workers. Chestnuts have been produced on the peninsula for a long time – well before potatoes, which were only "recently" imported from the Americas. As a result, chestnuts featured in many dishes, especially in the north. In order to have chestnuts available throughout the year, they were dried and, before use, were soaked for about 12 hours in just the same way as dried beans.

1 Put the beans, chestnuts and bay leaf in a pan, pour in 1 litre/1¾ pints/4 cups of water and bring to the boil. Lower the heat and cook for about 1½ hours, until tender.

2 Meanwhile, heat the oil in a frying pan. Add the onion and cook over a low heat, stirring occasionally, for 5 minutes, until softened. Add it to the soup. Season to taste with salt, remove and discard the bay leaf and mash the beans and chestnuts with a fork. Serve immediately.

SERVES 4

100g/3¾oz/ ½ cup dried haricot beans, soaked overnight in cold water and drained

90g/3½oz peeled chestnuts, thawed if frozen

1 bay leaf

50ml/2fl oz/¼ cup olive oil

1 onion, chopped

salt

COOK'S TIP

If using fresh chestnuts, do not store them for more than a week. The easiest way to shell them and remove their inner skins is to make a small cut in each one and par-boil or roast in the oven at 180°C/350°F/Gas 4 for about 5 minutes. Remove the shells and rub off the skins with a dish towel. Peeled frozen chestnuts are a simpler option.

VARIATION

You can also make this soup with fresh white beans in the summer.

PER PORTION Energy 184kcal/773kJ; Protein 6.2g; Carbohydrate 20.5g, of which sugars 3.1g; Fat 9.2g, of which saturates 1.4g; Cholesterol 0mg; Calcium 39mg; Fibre 5.1g; Sodium 8mg.

CORIANDER CREAM WITH FRESH CHEESE AND TOMATO CONFIT

CREME DE COENTROS COM QUEIJO FRESCO E TOMATE CONFITADO

This creamy soup is usually served warm, but it is just as delicious cold. It is the perfect choice as a chilled appetizer for an *al fresco* meal. Coriander is most popular in southern Portugal, where this soup originated.

1 Heat half the oil in a large pan. Add the onions, garlic and coriander and cook over a low heat, stirring occasionally, for 5 minutes, until softened.

2 Add the potatoes and 1 litre/1¾ pints/4 cups water. Bring to the boil, then lower the heat and cook for 20–30 minutes, until the potatoes are tender. Meanwhile, preheat the oven to 160°C/325°F/Gas 3.

3 Transfer the soup to a food processor or blender and process to a purée. Season to taste with salt. If you are serving the soup hot, reheat gently. Otherwise, leave to cool, then chill in the refrigerator.

4 Place the tomatoes in a small casserole, drizzle them with the remaining olive oil and season with salt and pepper. Bake the tomatoes in the oven for 10 minutes.

5 Serve the soup hot or cold in bowls with two tomatoes each, the cubed cheese and sprinkled with some of the olive oil used to cook the tomatoes.

SERVES 4

90ml/6 tbsp olive oil
3 onions, halved and sliced
1 garlic clove, chopped
2 bunches of fresh coriander (cilantro), about 300g/11oz, chopped
300g/11oz potatoes, diced
8 cherry tomatoes, peeled
150g/5oz fresh cheese, cut into cubes
salt and ground black pepper

VARIATION

If you choose to serve this soup hot, try replacing the fresh cheese with cubes of cured goat's cheese, warmed in the oven and sprinkled over at the last minute, as a delicious alternative.

PER PORTION Energy 353kcal/1467kJ; Protein 11.6g; Carbohydrate 23.6g, of which sugars 9.5g; Fat 24.3g, of which saturates 8.8g; Cholesterol 35mg; Calcium 137mg; Fibre 4g; Sodium 247mg.

TOMATO SOUP

TOMATADA

The bread makes this both a nourishing and substantial soup. The recipe originates in Alentejo, in southern Portugal, where poor people created fantastic soups simply with water and a combination of wild herbs and vegetables, such as coriander, asparagus, garlic, olive oil and, always, bread. On special occasions, they would add some goat's cheese or an egg. A simple, tasty dish for any occasion.

1 Heat the oil in a large pan. Add the onion and sausage and cook over a low heat, stirring occasionally, for 5 minutes, until the onion has softened. Add the garlic, tomatoes and oregano and cook for a further 5 minutes.

2 Pour in the stock or water, season to taste with salt, and cook, stirring frequently, until completely heated through.

3 Add the bread and coriander and cook, stirring, until the bread is fully incorporated. Serve immediately.

SERVES 4

50ml/2fl oz/¼ cup olive oil

1 onion, chopped

1 small sausage, preferably from black pork, cut into small pieces

1 garlic clove, chopped

4 ripe tomatoes, peeled, seeded and diced

1 fresh oregano sprig

1 litre/1¾ pints/4 cups chicken stock or water

4 small slices of dry bread, cut into cubes

15ml/1 tbsp chopped fresh coriander (cilantro)

salt

COOK'S TIPS

• To peel a tomato, cut a cross in the top, immerse in boiling water for 1 minute and refresh in iced water. Then peel off the skin.

• You can add a poached egg to each bowl just before serving.

PER PORTION Energy 233kcal/971kJ; Protein 5.4g; Carbohydrate 19.1g, of which sugars 4.9g; Fat 15.5g, of which saturates 3.6g; Cholesterol 9mg; Calcium 50mg; Fibre 1.7g; Sodium 695mg.

SERVES 4–8

4 dogfish fillets, about 4cm/1½ in thick, or about 150g/5oz each

75ml/5 tbsp olive oil

2 garlic cloves, chopped

1 bunch of fresh coriander (cilantro), chopped

1 bay leaf

50ml/2fl oz/¼ cup white wine vinegar

15ml/1 tbsp plain (all-purpose) flour

salt

For the marinade

1 bay leaf

50ml/2fl oz white wine vinegar

salt

VARIATION

This soup can also be made with swordfish or shark fillets.

DOGFISH SOUP

SOPA DE CAÇÃO

Dogfish, a member of the shark family, is found along the Alentejo coast, where this soup is very popular. This fish is also known as huss, flake, tope and rock salmon. This recipe is sufficient for a meal-in-a-bowl soup for four or, alternatively, a first course for eight.

1 First, make the marinade by combining all the ingredients with 500ml/7fl oz/2 cups water in a jug (pitcher). Place the fish fillets in a dish and pour the marinade over them. Leave to marinate for at least 2 hours, then rinse in water.

2 Heat the olive oil in a large pan. Add the garlic and coriander and cook, stirring, for a few minutes. Pour in 1 litre/1¾ pints/4 cups water, add the fish and the bay leaf, and season with salt. Bring to the boil, then lower the heat and simmer for 10 minutes. Reserve the fish and throw away the bay leaf.

3 Mix together the vinegar and flour and blend into the soup. Simmer for about 10 minutes, stirring until the flour is combined, and add more water if necessary. Add the fish and serve immediately.

PER PORTION Energy 174kcal/724kJ; Protein 18.8g; Carbohydrate 2.2g, of which sugars 0.2g; Fat 10g, of which saturates 1.4g; Cholesterol 46mg; Calcium 29mg; Fibre 0.5g; Sodium 63mg.

SERVES 6

60ml/4 tbsp olive oil

2kg/4½ lb prawn (shrimp) heads and fish bones

1kg/2¼ lb mixed onions, carrots, leek, and garlic, coarsely chopped

1 bay leaf

6 black peppercorns

105ml/7 tbsp dry white wine

1 green and 1 red (bell) pepper, seeded and finely diced

1 onion, chopped

2 ripe tomatoes, peeled and diced

1 garlic clove, chopped

15ml/1 tbsp chopped fresh thyme

185g/6½ oz live clams, scrubbed

125g/4¼ oz prepared squid

300g/11oz white fish fillet, cut into chunks

12 prawns (shrimp), peeled

chopped fresh coriander (cilantro), to garnish

PER PORTION Energy 267kcal/1112kJ; Protein 20.1g; Carbohydrate 25.2g, of which sugars 18.7g; Fat 9g, of which saturates 1.3g; Cholesterol 96mg; Calcium 96mg; Fibre 4.8g; Sodium 262mg.

SEAFOOD SOUP

SOPA DO MAR

Rich seafood soups are prepared in a variety of ways all along the coast of Portugal. Whenever you prepare a dish with prawns or fillet fish, save the heads and bones and freeze them until you have enough to make a flavoursome stock, such as the one used in this recipe. Some versions of this seafood soup add diced potato to the stock, while others add rice or noodles. The soup can be served simply with fresh bread.

1 Heat 30ml/2 tbsp of the olive oil in a large pan. Add the prawn heads and cook over a low heat, stirring frequently, for 5 minutes.

2 Add the mixed vegetables, bay leaf and peppercorns and cook for a further 5 minutes, mashing the prawn heads with a wooden spoon.

3 Pour in the wine and 2 litres/3½ pints/8¾ cups water. Bring to the boil, then lower the heat and simmer gently for 1 hour.

4 Add the fish bones and bring back to the boil. Lower the heat and simmer very gently for 20 minutes. Remove the pan from the heat and strain the stock into a bowl.

5 Heat the remaining olive oil in a large, clean pan. Add the green and red peppers, onion and tomatoes, and cook over a low heat, stirring occasionally, for 5 minutes, until softened. Add the garlic and thyme, pour in the stock and bring just to the boil.

6 Add the clams and squid and cook for 2–3 minutes, until the clams have opened. Add the fish and prawns and cook for 5 minutes more, until the fish is opaque. Sprinkle with the coriander and serve immediately.

CORN SOUP WITH COCKLES

XARÉM DE BERBIGÃO

The basis of this soup is coarse cornmeal, which is left over after fine cornmeal has been produced. Poor people used to collect these "leftovers" from the miller, and would mix them with whatever seafood they could find along the shore. This traditional recipe is from the Algarve, in the south of Portugal. Coarse cornmeal is also used in other regions, but usually in combination with meat, or even as a dessert mixed with sugar and egg yolks.

1 Wash the cockles thoroughly and discard any with broken shells. Bring the water or stock to the boil, add the cockles and cook for about 4–5 minutes until they open.

2 Discard any cockles that remain closed. Strain the cooking liquid through a fine sieve (strainer) into a bowl and reserve. Set the cockles aside.

3 Heat the olive oil in a large pan, add the onion and cook over a low heat, stirring occasionally, for 5 minutes, until softened.

4 Add the reserved cooking liquid to the pan and sprinkle in the cornmeal or semolina, stirring constantly.

5 Simmer for 5 minutes, and then add the cockles and parsley and heat through briefly. Pour into a warmed tureen and serve immediately.

SERVES 4

300g/11oz live cockles
1 litre/1¾ pints/4 cups water or light chicken stock
50ml/2fl oz/¼ cup olive oil
1 onion, finely chopped
150g/5oz/1¼ cups coarse cornmeal or semolina
30ml/2 tbsp chopped fresh parsley

COOK'S TIP

Make sure that you buy cockles from a reputable supplier and cook them on the day of purchase. It is unwise to collect them from the beach because of the high risk of pollution.

VARIATION

Live cockles are not widely available from fish stores. You can substitute mussels or small clams in this recipe.

PER PORTION Energy 240kcal/999kJ; Protein 8.4g; Carbohydrate 28.8g, of which sugars 1g; Fat 9.8g, of which saturates 1.3g; Cholesterol 20mg; Calcium 52mg; Fibre 1.4g; Sodium 186mg.

SERVES 6

1 hare or rabbit
2 carrots
75ml/5 tbsp olive oil
75ml/5 tbsp dry white port
1 onion, sliced
1 leek, sliced
1 garlic clove, chopped
6 black peppercorns
1 bay leaf
15ml/1 tbsp cornflour (cornstarch)
1 turnip, diced
3 heads pak choi (bok choy), cut into strips
200g/7oz oyster mushrooms, sliced
300g/11oz/2¼ cups cooked haricot beans
1 small bunch of fresh peppermint, chopped
salt

COOK'S TIP

For ease of cooking, ask your butcher to portion your hare or rabbit for you.

PER PORTION Energy 297kcal/1242kJ; Protein 24g; Carbohydrate 18.7g, of which sugars 8.5g; Fat 12.9g, of which saturates 2.9g; Cholesterol 69mg; Calcium 159mg; Fibre 6.4g; Sodium 299mg.

HARE SOUP
SOPA DE LEBRE

This rich soup is a great favourite in the centre and south of Portugal. Served with fresh bread, it is a meal in itself. The soup can be made with other game, such as pheasant, and the white beans can be replaced with lentils, which combine excellently with game. If available, use wild peppermint for its pronounced aroma and flavour.

1 Cut the hare into pieces. Wash well and pat dry with kitchen paper. Slice one carrot and dice the other. Heat 45ml/3 tbsp of the olive oil in a large pan. Add the pieces of hare and cook, turning occasionally, for about 10 minutes, until golden brown all over.

2 Drain off the oil from the pan. Add the port, onion, leek, sliced carrot, garlic, peppercorns and bay leaf, and pour in enough water to cover. Bring to the boil, then lower the heat and simmer gently for 1½ hours.

3 Strain the stock into a bowl and reserve the meat. Remove the bones from the meat and cut the meat into small pieces. Return the stock to the rinsed-out pan and set over a low heat.

4 Mix the cornflour to a paste with 30ml/2 tbsp water. Stir it into the stock and season to taste with salt.

5 Cook the remaining carrot, the turnip and pak choi in separate pans of boiling water until just tender, then add to the stock.

6 Meanwhile, heat the remaining oil in another pan, add the mushrooms and cook over a low heat, stirring occasionally, for 5–7 minutes. Add them to the stock with the beans. Stir in the reserved meat and the peppermint, heat through gently and serve.

FISH & SHELLFISH

Rich supplies of freshwater and sea fish and shellfish are found throughout Portugal – choose from grilled (broiled) fish, mixed seafood stew, fish risotto or the region's favourite *bacalhau*, or salted cod.

FISH AND SHELLFISH are staple ingredients in a country with such a large unpolluted coastal area. The cold currents flowing down the Portuguese coast bring fish of excellent quality, and the deep waters around the islands of Madeira and the Azores are also rich in fish such as tuna and swordfish, stone bass and bream. Sardines are a whole industry in themselves, sold fresh or preserved with tomato or olive oil.

The best quality fish from the sea is simply grilled (broiled) with a dash of lemon and olive oil, or served with a richer dressing of tomatoes, onions, peppers and aromatic herbs, or covered with butter and chopped parsley.

The lesser cuts are not forgotten – nothing is wasted in the thrifty cuisine of Portugal. One favourite dish is *caldeirada*, a kind of stew composed of a combination of different fish: golden bream, ray, sardine, squid and more, cooked with tomatoes, red (bell) peppers, onions, sliced potatoes and a dash of garlic, pepper, parsley and paprika, in a stock made of white wine and water. Each coastal town tends to have its own recipe, a variation on the theme of fish, vegetables and wine.

Portugal's rivers are a fine source of freshwater fish. Lamprey is a speciality of the river Minho, in the north of Portugal, usually prepared with red wine; in the Douro region, further south, a touch of port wine is added, giving a very different taste. Shad is prepared in *escabeche* (a vinegar and onion dressing poured over the cooked fish), or cut very thinly and fried, and then served with soft bread mashed with the roes.

Fish blends superbly with rice in a risotto-like creamy dish, *arroz de marisco* (seafood rice), using any available local fish. The rice is served *malandrinho*, which means it is cooked with lots of water so that it is really juicy. Rice and potatoes are often served as an accompaniment to grilled fish, with chopped vegetables or salad.

There are many recipes for *bacalhau* (salted cod). Not for nothing is it known as "the faithful friend". This rather solid, strong-tasting fish may be an acquired taste, but its salty flavour goes well with mashed potatoes in *bacalhau à Conde da Guarda*, and with a crust of corn bread in *bacalhau com broa*.

SALT COD WITH SCRAMBLED EGGS, ONION AND POTATOES

BACALHAU À BRÁS

This succulent salt cod dish is a recipe that originates from the Lisbon region. Bacalhau à Brás is the classic Portuguese way to prepare cod. Thin strips of cod are combined with onions, alongside a mixture of thin strips of potatoes and scrambled eggs.

1 Bring a pan of water to the boil. Add the fish and bring back to the boil, then immediately remove the pan from the heat. Leave to stand for 5 minutes.

2 Remove the fish from the pan with a slotted spatula and leave to cool slightly. Remove and discard the skin and bones.

3 Heat the olive oil in a large pan. Add the onions and cook over a low heat, stirring occasionally, for 5 minutes, until softened. Add the fish, then the potatoes and, finally, the beaten eggs. Stir gently until all the ingredients are thoroughly combined but the eggs are still soft. Serve the dish immediately, sprinkled with the parsley and olives.

SERVES 4

400g/14oz salt cod, soaked
50ml/2fl oz/¼ cup olive oil
3 onions, thinly sliced
500g/1¼lb potatoes, cut into thin matchsticks (julienne) and deep-fried
8 eggs, lightly beaten
1 small bunch of parsley, chopped
12 black olives

VARIATION

Another recipe called Bacalhau à Gomes de Sá originates in Porto (Oporto), and has the same ingredients but a different preparation technique. In this dish, the onions are cooked in olive oil, and mixed with cooked potatoes and salt cod marinated in milk. The dish is then served with parsley, cooked eggs and black olives.

PER PORTION Energy 484kcal/2032kJ; Protein 49.1g; Carbohydrate 30.4g, of which sugars 8.9g; Fat 19.7g, of which saturates 4.4g; Cholesterol 440mg; Calcium 151mg; Fibre 4g; Sodium 843mg.

SERVES 8

1kg/2¼ lb potatoes, unpeeled
800g/1¾ lb salt cod, soaked
105ml/7 tbsp olive oil
200ml/7fl oz/scant 1 cup single (light) cream
2 garlic cloves, chopped
1 small bunch of parsley, chopped
pinch of freshly grated nutmeg
salt

PER PORTION Energy 366kcal/1535kJ; Protein 35.9g; Carbohydrate 21.4g, of which sugars 2.4g; Fat 15.8g, of which saturates 4.7g; Cholesterol 73mg; Calcium 65mg; Fibre 1.7g; Sodium 423mg.

SALT COD WITH POTATO MASH GRATIN

BACALHAU À CONDE DA GUARDA

This recipe is reminiscent of the well-known French salt cod purée, *brandade*. Many similar dishes are produced in other Mediterranean countries, using salt or dried cod, which is also known as stockfish. Serve with an assortment of lettuce, seasoned with parsley vinaigrette. A smaller portion of this recipe is ideal as an appetizer.

1 Cook the potatoes in a large pan of lightly salted boiling water for 20–30 minutes, until tender. Drain well, then peel and mash with a fork. Meanwhile, preheat the oven to 200°C/400°F/Gas 6.

2 Bring another large pan of water to the boil. Add the fish and bring back to the boil, then immediately remove the pan from the heat. Leave to stand for 5 minutes.

3 Remove the fish from the pan with a slotted spatula and leave to cool slightly. Remove and discard the skin and bones.

4 Mix the fish with the potatoes, then blend in the olive oil and cream and the garlic. Stir in the parsley and nutmeg and season with salt, if necessary. Spoon the mixture into an ovenproof dish and bake for about 20 minutes. Serve hot.

SALT COD PANCAKES WITH JUICY CABBAGE RICE

PATANISCAS DE BACALHAU COM ARROZ DE COUVE

This dish is prepared all over Portugal; in some regions, the fish is cut into small pieces, in others, cooks use the whole fillet. The rice can be prepared with several kinds of vegetables, with favourites being turnip tops, kidney beans and tomatoes.

1 Remove the skin and bones from the fish and place the fillets in a dish. Mix together 300ml/½ pint/1¼ cups of the milk and lemon juice and pour over the fish. Leave to marinate for 30 minutes.

2 Beat the egg with the olive oil in a bowl. Stir in the flour, onion, parsley and enough of the remaining milk to make a medium-thick paste.

3 Meanwhile, prepare the juicy cabbage rice. Heat the olive oil in a large pan. Add the onion and garlic and cook over a low heat, stirring occasionally, for 5 minutes, until softened.

4 Add the rice and cook, stirring frequently, for 1–2 minutes, until the grains are coated with oil. Pour in 750ml/1¼ pints/3 cups water and bring to the boil. Add the cabbage and season with salt. Cook for 15–20 minutes, until the rice is just tender.

5 Meanwhile, heat the oil for deep-frying to 180–190°C/350–375°F or until a cube of day-old bread browns in 40 seconds. Remove the fish fillets from the marinade and pass them through the paste to coat. Add to the hot oil and deep-fry for 5–7 minutes, until golden brown. Remove with a slotted spatula and drain on kitchen paper, then serve with the rice.

SERVES 4

400g/14oz salt cod, soaked
450ml/¾ pint/scant 2 cups milk
15ml/1 tbsp lemon juice
1 large (US extra large) egg
20ml/4 tsp olive oil
100g/3¾oz/scant 1 cup plain (all-purpose) flour
1 small onion, finely chopped
1 small bunch of parsley, chopped
vegetable oil, for deep-frying

For the juicy cabbage rice
30ml/2 tbsp olive oil
1 onion, chopped
1 garlic clove, chopped
250g/9oz/1¼ cups risotto rice
1 small cabbage, cored and shredded
salt

VARIATIONS

• To give the rice extra flavour, cook it in stock instead of water.
• An alternative to cabbage rice is to add diced bacon or sausage and/or cubed tomato to the onion in the pan.

PER PORTION Energy 687kcal/2874kJ; Protein 43.4g; Carbohydrate 77.6g, of which sugars 7.9g; Fat 22.9g, of which saturates 3.4g; Cholesterol 107mg; Calcium 164mg; Fibre 4.2g; Sodium 431mg.

SERVES 4

150ml/¼ pint/⅔ cup olive oil, plus extra for brushing
300g/11oz/6 cups corn bread crumbs
30ml/2 tbsp chopped fresh parsley
1 garlic clove, finely chopped
15ml/1 tbsp sweet paprika
4 pieces of salt cod cut from the centre, about 200g/7oz each
cooked cabbage and baked potatoes, to serve

COOK'S TIP

To prepare baked potatoes the Portuguese way, make a layer of sea salt on a baking tray. Place 2–3 medium young potatoes per serving on top and cover them with sea salt. Bake in a preheated oven at 180°C/350°F/Gas 4 for about 1 hour. Check to see how soft they are by inserting a wooden cocktail stick (toothpick). If necessary, cook them for a little longer. Transfer the potatoes to a serving dish, shaking off the salt, press with your hand so they break open and sprinkle with olive oil.

SALT COD WITH A CORN BREAD CRUST

BACALHAU COM BROA

The centre part of salt cod, preferably from an adult fish, provides the plump fillet that is most prized in Portugal. The classic way to serve it is chargrilled and then drizzled with plenty of olive oil. Another option is to add seafood, such as shrimp and clams. In this delicious recipe, the corn bread crust protects the cod from drying out, retaining all its juices and flavour.

1 Preheat the oven to 200°C/400°F/Gas 6. Brush a shallow ovenproof dish with oil.

2 Mix together the breadcrumbs, parsley, garlic, paprika and olive oil to a thick paste in a bowl. (You may not need all the oil.)

3 Spread this paste all over the fish, place in the prepared dish and bake for about 20 minutes. Serve immediately with cabbage and baked potatoes.

PER PORTION Energy 781kcal/3290kJ; Protein 74.6g; Carbohydrate 59.8g, of which sugars 2.2g; Fat 28.9g, of which saturates 4.1g; Cholesterol 118mg; Calcium 173mg; Fibre 2.3g; Sodium 1376mg.

ROASTED SEA BREAM
PARGO ASSADO NO FORNO

This is a classic way of cooking a whole fish. The sauce is juicy and combines superbly with the taste of the bream. You can use other fish instead of sea bream, but red bream is essential to make the most of this delicious dish. It is traditional to cook the fish whole, but you can also roast individual portions using the same method.

1 Preheat the oven to 180°C/350°F/Gas 4. Using a sharp knife, slash the fish twice on each side. Place it in a large, shallow ovenproof dish or roasting pan, drizzle with 60ml/ 4 tbsp of the olive oil and sprinkle with sea salt. Place in the oven and roast for about 10 minutes, until half cooked.

2 Meanwhile, heat the remaining oil in a frying pan. Add the onions, garlic and bay leaves and cook over a low heat, stirring occasionally, for 5 minutes, until the onions are soft and translucent. Add the tomatoes and the wine and simmer gently to warm through.

3 When the fish has been in the oven for 10 minutes, spoon the onion mixture over it, return to the oven and roast for a further 10 minutes. Transfer to a serving dish, sprinkle with the parsley and serve immediately with cooked potatoes and vegetables.

SERVES 4

1 red bream or porgy, weighing 1.6–2kg/3½–4½lb, scaled and cleaned

105ml/7 tbsp olive oil

2 onions, sliced

2 garlic cloves, chopped

2 bay leaves

2 ripe tomatoes, peeled and diced

50ml/2fl oz/¼ cup white wine

sea salt

chopped fresh parsley, to garnish

potatoes and vegetables, to serve

PER PORTION Energy 403kcal/1679kJ; Protein 32.5g; Carbohydrate 11.5g, of which sugars 8.6g; Fat 24.7g, of which saturates 2.8g; Cholesterol 67mg; Calcium 106mg; Fibre 2.3g; Sodium 201mg.

HAKE WITH TURNIP TOPS AND ONIONS

PESCADA À POVEIRA

This recipe comes from Povoa de Varzim, a fishing harbour north of Porto. Hake is highly prized in the north and served in many different ways. A member of the cod family, it has a deliciously soft texture and an excellent flavour, but should be handled carefully as it is quite fragile.

1 Preheat the oven to 180°C/350°F/Gas 4. Heat 30ml/2 tbsp of the olive oil in a flameproof casserole. Add the onions, garlic, paprika and bay leaf and cook over a low heat, stirring occasionally, for 5 minutes, until the onions have softened.

2 Add the vinegar and the stock or water, then place the hake in the casserole and season with salt. Cover and cook in the oven for 15 minutes.

3 Meanwhile, steam the turnip tops or cook in a little boiling water for 3–5 minutes, then drain if necessary. Press them through a sieve (strainer) into a bowl, mix with 15ml/1 tbsp of the remaining olive oil and keep warm.

4 Peel the potatoes and cut into quarters. Heat the remaining olive oil in a sauté pan or frying pan, add the potatoes and cook over a medium-low heat, turning occasionally, for 7–8 minutes until light golden brown.

5 Using a slotted spatula, transfer the fish to a large serving plate. Add the potatoes, turnip tops and eggs and spoon over the onion sauce. Serve immediately.

SERVES 4

105ml/7 tbsp olive oil
2 small onions, chopped
2 garlic cloves, chopped
5ml/1 tsp sweet paprika
1 bay leaf
15ml/1 tbsp white vine vinegar
150ml/¼ pint/⅔ cup fish stock or water
4 hake steaks, about 225g/8oz each
200g/7oz turnip tops (the green part of the turnip)
8 potatoes, boiled without peeling
4 hard-boiled eggs, halved
salt

COOK'S TIP

Turnip tops have a delicious, slightly bitter taste. Be careful not to overcook them. If they are not used immediately, plunge into ice water to keep the colour and reheat, with olive oil, when needed.

PER PORTION Energy 614kcal/2571kJ; Protein 51g; Carbohydrate 36.2g, of which sugars 5.7g; Fat 30.7g, of which saturates 5.2g; Cholesterol 242mg; Calcium 102mg; Fibre 3.4g; Sodium 326mg.

LISBON FISH MOULD
PUDIM DE PESCADA À LISBOETA

This dish, served in a mould, comes from the capital city of Lisbon. Using bread instead of the more usual flour makes it lighter. Vary the recipe by adding shrimps and fresh herbs, such as chives, parsley or chervil.

1 Preheat the oven to 160°C/325°F/Gas 3. Grease an ovenproof round mould and a round of baking parchment. Process the fish in a food processor until smooth. Set aside.

2 Tear the bread into pieces and place in a large pan. Add half the milk and cook over a low heat, stirring constantly and gradually adding more milk, until a smooth thick paste forms. Remove the pan from the heat.

3 Stir in the fish, butter and egg yolks and season with salt and pepper. Whisk the egg whites in a grease-free bowl until stiff, then fold into the fish mixture. Spoon the mixture into the prepared mould and cover with the baking parchment. Place in a roasting pan, add boiling water to come halfway up the sides and cook in the oven for 45 minutes.

4 Meanwhile, scrub the mussels under cold running water and pull off the beards. Discard any with broken shells or that do not shut immediately when sharply tapped. Place them in a pan with 50ml/2fl oz/¼ cup water, cover and bring to the boil over a high heat. Cook, shaking the pan occasionally, for 4–5 minutes, until the shells have opened. Drain and discard any that remain closed. Turn out the mould on to a warm serving dish and serve with the mussels.

SERVES 6–8

300g/11oz/1⅓ cups butter, at room temperature, plus extra for greasing

1kg/2¼ lb hake fillets, skinned and cut into pieces

300g/11oz crustless dry white bread

300ml/½ pint/1¼ cups milk

6 eggs, separated

800g/1¾ lb live mussels

salt and ground black pepper

VARIATION

Replace the hake with other white fish, such as cod or haddock, or salmon.

PER PORTION Energy 581kcal/2420kJ; Protein 37g; Carbohydrate 20.5g, of which sugars 3g; Fat 39.7g, of which saturates 21.6g; Cholesterol 266mg; Calcium 191mg; Fibre 0.6g; Sodium 679mg.

SERVES 4

200g/7oz live clams
600g/1lb 6oz monkfish fillet
1 bunch of coriander (cilantro), chopped
2 garlic cloves, chopped
105ml/7 tbsp fish stock
50ml/2fl oz/¼ cup olive oil
white bread, to serve

VARIATION

You can also add chopped onion, seeded
and diced (bell) pepper and even some
sliced sausage to this dish.

PER PORTION Energy 193kcal/809kJ; Protein 27g;
Carbohydrate 0.7g, of which sugars 0.3g; Fat 9.2g, of
which saturates 1.4g; Cholesterol 34mg; Calcium 51mg;
Fibre 0.6g; Sodium 297mg.

MONKFISH WITH CLAMS AND CORIANDER

TAMBORIL COM AMÊIJOAS E COENTROS

This dish, from southern Portugal, is usually prepared in a pan called a
cataplana. Made of copper, the *cataplana* looks like two lids that seal tightly
together. Once placed on the heat, it allows even cooking and retains all the
steam. It is used for many Portuguese dishes, especially fish and shellfish.

1 Scrub the clams under cold running water. Discard any with broken shells or that do
not shut when sharply tapped.

2 Put the clams and all the other ingredients in a large pan with a tight-fitting lid. Cover
the pan and cook over a medium heat for 15 minutes.

3 Remove and discard any clams that have not opened. Serve immediately with slices
of white bread.

GROUPER STEWED WITH GRAPES

CHERNE COM UVAS COMO NO "MOLHO DE PEIXE"

Fish stews are found in all Mediterranean cuisines and in other coastal regions of southern Europe. This one, originating from the Atlantic islands of the Azores, has an original touch as it uses green grapes, which add an elegant acidity to the flavour.

1 Preheat the oven to 180°C/350°F/Gas 4. Heat the oil in a flameproof casserole. Add the onion, garlic, green pepper and bay leaf and cook over a low heat, stirring occasionally, for 5 minutes, until the onion has softened.

2 Add the tomato and saffron and cook for a few minutes more, then add the grapes and stock and bring to the boil.

3 Place the fish in the casserole, skin side up, cover and cook in the oven for about 20 minutes, until the fish is cooked through and tender. Sprinkle with the mint and serve immediately.

SERVES 4

50ml/2fl oz/¼ cup olive oil

1 small onion, chopped

1 garlic clove, chopped

1 green (bell) pepper, seeded and chopped

1 bay leaf

1 ripe tomato, peeled and diced

5ml/1 tsp saffron threads

20 green grapes

200ml/7fl oz/scant 1 cup fish stock

4 grouper fillets with skin, each weighing about 175g/6oz

1 small bunch of mint, chopped

PER PORTION Energy 248kcal/1037kJ; Protein 33.2g; Carbohydrate 6.7g, of which sugars 6.1g; Fat 9.9g, of which saturates 1.4g; Cholesterol 81mg; Calcium 51mg; Fibre 1.9g; Sodium 114mg.

FISH & SHELLFISH **75**

SERVES 4

500g/1¼lb raw prawns (shrimp), in their shells

4 tiger prawns (jumbo shrimp), about 140g/4¾oz each, in their shells

150ml/¼ pint/⅔ cup olive oil

5ml/1 tsp sweet paprika

500g/1¼lb dry white bread, crusts removed and cut into cubes

3 garlic cloves, finely chopped

piri piri or Tabasco sauce, to taste

45ml/3 tbsp chopped fresh parsley or fresh coriander (cilantro)

2 egg yolks

For the shellfish stock

150ml/¼ pint/⅔ cup olive oil

2 onions, quartered

1 leek, cut in small pieces

3 carrots, cubed

3 garlic cloves, chopped

1 bunch of parsley

3 bay leaves

6 grains of black pepper

250ml/8fl oz/1 cup white wine

500ml/17fl oz/generous 2 cups fresh tomato juice

2kg/4½lb shrimp heads and shells

PER PORTION Energy 640kcal/2688kJ; Protein 27.5g; Carbohydrate 62.7g, of which sugars 3.6g; Fat 32.8g, of which saturates 4.9g; Cholesterol 319mg; Calcium 253mg; Fibre 2.5g; Sodium 2232mg.

PRAWN AND BREAD MASH WITH PAN-FRIED TIGER PRAWNS

AÇORDA DE CAMARÃO COM CAMARÃO TIGRE GRELHADO

Bread soups are associated with fish and shellfish, especially salt cod and prawns. Served as a main dish, the flavour is strong, but using the "soup" as a garnish for grilled seafood offers a pleasant, complementary flavour.

1 Cook the prawns in salted boiling water for 2–3 minutes. Drain, refresh in cold water and drain again. Pull off the heads and peel the prawns, reserving the heads and shells. Set aside. Peel the tiger prawns, keeping the heads on, reserving the shells. Set aside.

2 For the shellfish stock heat the oil in a big pot and fry the shrimp heads and shells for about 10 minutes, stirring occasionally. Then mash the mixture. Add the vegetables, blend and add the rest of the ingredients. Cover with 3–5 litres/5–7 pints of water and cook for 2 hours. Pass the stock through a sieve (strainer).

3 In a pan, fry the tiger prawns in 45ml/3 tbsp of olive oil, sprinkle with the paprika and fry for 2 minutes on each side. Add some stock and return to the heat for 2–3 minutes.

4 Put the bread, shellfish stock, garlic and remaining olive oil in a pan and cook over a medium heat, stirring constantly, for 5 minutes, until the mixture is smooth but not too dry. Add the reserved prawns, *piri piri* or Tabasco to taste, and the parsley. Stir in the egg yolks. Serve the bread mash with the pan-fried tiger prawns and the sauce.

STUFFED SQUID

LULAS RECHEADAS

Characteristic to most of the Portuguese coast, the preparation of this recipe can vary considerably. The squid meat can be replaced by squid tentacles. The stuffing can also be prepared with other fish, such as hake, as long as you leave out the tomato in the stuffing.

1 Rinse the squid under cold running water, then pull the head away from the body – the entrails will come away with the head. Cut off the tentacles and squeeze out the beak. Chop the tentacles and discard the beak. Pull out and discard the transparent quill from the body sac and clean out any remaining membrane. Rinse the body sac and peel off the skin.

2 Heat 50ml/2fl oz/¼ cup of the olive oil in a pan. Add half the onions and half the garlic and cook over a low heat, stirring occasionally, for 5 minutes, until softened. Add the chopped tentacles, ham and sausage or bacon and cook for a few minutes more. Stir in about a quarter of the tomatoes and all the rice. Mix well and remove the pan from the heat.

3 Spoon the filling into the body sacs of the squid, filling them just over half full. Secure the openings with wooden cocktail sticks (toothpicks).

4 Heat the remaining oil in a large pan. Add the remaining onions and garlic and cook over a low heat, stirring occasionally, for 5 minutes, until softened. Add the bay leaf and remaining tomatoes and pour in about 150ml/¼ pint/⅔ cup water to top up. Stir in the parsley and add the stuffed squid. Season with salt and simmer gently for about 20 minutes, until tender. Serve with cooked potatoes.

SERVES 4

1kg/2¼lb squid, preferably about 10cm/4in long
150ml/¼ pint/⅔ cup olive oil
4 onions, chopped
2 garlic cloves, chopped
100g/3¾oz cured ham, chopped
150g/5oz sausage or bacon, chopped
4 large ripe tomatoes, peeled and chopped
100g/3¾oz/generous ½ cup cooked rice
1 bay leaf
1 bunch of parsley, chopped
salt
cooked potatoes, to serve

VARIATION

As an alternative to stewing the squid, try them grilled (broiled) with a little olive oil and sprinkled with the chopped parsley.

PER PORTION 715kcal/2987kJ; Protein 50.8g; Carbohydrate 33.5g, of which sugars 15.1g; Fat 43.1g, of which saturates 9.6g; Cholesterol 595mg; Calcium 111mg; Fibre 4g; Sodium 875mg.

JUICY SEAFOOD RICE
ARROZ DE MARISCO

All along the coast from north to south, any restaurant will serve this rice dish, made with the best produce the sea can supply. It is often served in the pan in which it is cooked, or in a terracotta pot placed in the centre of the table and shared by everyone. The rice used is carolino rice, which is similar to Italian risotto rice, but long grain rice is a good alternative.

1 Heat the olive oil in a large pan. Add the onion and green pepper and cook over a low heat, stirring occasionally, for 5 minutes, until softened. Add the tomato and the stock and bring to the boil.

2 Open the clams, cockles and mussels. The easiest way do this is by steaming them briefly in a little water and removing them from their shells as soon as they open. It's best to do this in small batches. Reserve the shellfish meat, keeping the shells to one side.

3 Add the rice to the pan, bring back to the boil and cook for about 12 minutes, until tender. The mixture should be moist; if necessary, add more stock. Add all the seafood and the coriander, heat through briefly and serve, decorated with the seafood shells.

SERVES 4

50ml/2fl oz/¼ cup olive oil

1 onion, chopped

1 green (bell) pepper, seeded and chopped

1 tomato, peeled and chopped

1 litre/1¾ pints/4 cups shellfish stock

200g/7oz live clams, scrubbed

200g/7oz live cockles, scrubbed

200g/7oz live mussels, scrubbed and beards removed

300g/11oz/generous 1½ cups risotto rice

400g/14oz cooked peeled prawns (shrimp)

30ml/2 tbsp chopped fresh coriander (cilantro)

PER PORTION Energy 484kcal/2027kJ; Protein 32g; Carbohydrate 64.6g, of which sugars 4.2g; Fat 10.5g, of which saturates 1.5g; Cholesterol 213mg; Calcium 215mg; Fibre 1.7g; Sodium 292mg.

SERVES 4

1kg/2½ lb eel fillets, cut into 4cm/
1½ in slices

500g/1¼ lb potatoes, cut into 5mm/
¼ in slices

2 onions, very thinly sliced

2 bay leaves, torn into pieces

2 garlic cloves, chopped

50ml/2fl oz/¼ cup white wine

105ml/7 tbsp olive oil

1 bunch of parsley, chopped

5–7.5ml/1–1½ tsp ground ginger

salt

bread, to serve

VARIATIONS

• You can add some green and red
(bell) pepper between the layers.

• The eels can also be cooked in 4cm/
1½ in boned pieces, in which case make
the potato slices thicker as the eel will
take longer to cook.

PER PORTION Energy 738kcal/3074kJ; Protein 45.5g;
Carbohydrate 30.4g, of which sugars 9g; Fat 48.3g, of
which saturates 10.1g; Cholesterol 375mg; Calcium
113mg; Fibre 3.6g; Sodium 245mg.

EEL STEW

CALDEIRADA DE ENGUIAS

One excellent way to cook eel is in *escabeche*, when it is poached or fried
and then marinated, but eel stew is another popular option. Different regions
of Portugal cook this stew with a variety of other fish. One common method
is to combine several types of fish, such as sardines, skate or conger eel.

1 If you haven't asked your fishmonger to prepare the eels, prepare them yourself by
cutting off the heads and sprinkling the skin with salt so you can pull it off. Then rinse
them well in cold running water.

2 Make a layer of potatoes in a large pan, then make a layer of onions, followed by a
layer of fish. Season with pieces of bay leaf, some garlic, a little wine and olive oil and a
sprinkling of parsley, ginger and salt. Continue making layers in this way until all the
ingredients have been used up.

3 Sprinkle in 100ml/3½ fl oz/scant ½ cup water, cover and cook on a low heat
for about 30 minutes, until the fish is cooked through and the vegetables are tender.
Serve with bread.

SERVES 4

1 octopus, about 1.6kg/3½ lb

150ml/¼ pint/⅔ cup olive oil

2 onions, chopped

300g/11oz/generous 1½ cups long grain rice

1 bay leaf

For the stock

2 onions, quartered

1 leek, chopped

3 garlic cloves, crushed

10 black peppercorns

2 bay leaves

pinch of salt

COOK'S TIP

A way of tenderizing the octopus is to store it in the freezer and then thaw it overnight in the refrigerator.

PER PORTION Energy 871kcal/3646kJ; Protein 78.8g; Carbohydrate 69.7g, of which sugars 7g; Fat 30.9g, of which saturates 4.8g; Cholesterol 192mg; Calcium 178mg; Fibre 1.8g; Sodium 95mg.

BRAISED OCTOPUS WITH RICE
POLVO ASSADO COM ARROZ NO FORNO

While it has a delicate flavour, octopus also has a reputation for being chewy. This texture largely depends on its origin and quality, but also on how it is cooked. Nowadays, octopus is usually sold already blanched and tenderized, but this recipe describes the method for cooking fresh octopus.

1 Rinse the octopus in plenty of water and cut off the body. Turn the body inside out and pull out and discard the entrails. Remove the little strips from the sides of the body. Rinse thoroughly again and turn the right way out. Squeeze out the beak. Beat the tentacles lightly with a rolling pin or the flat side of a meat mallet.

2 Half fill a large pan with water and add all the ingredients for the stock. Bring to the boil, then lower the heat and simmer for 10 minutes.

3 Add the octopus and bring back to the boil. Lower the heat slightly so that the liquid continues to boil and cook for 1 hour. Check with a fork to see if the octopus is tender. If not, cook for a little longer but check frequently because it will toughen if overcooked.

4 Strain the stock into a bowl and reserve. Discard the flavourings. Chop the octopus body and cut the tentacles into short lengths, keeping the two parts separate. Preheat the oven to 160°C/325°F/Gas 3.

5 Heat 50ml/2fl oz/¼ cup of the olive oil in a flameproof casserole. Add the onions and cook over a low heat, stirring occasionally, for 10 minutes, until lightly browned. Add the rice, the octopus body, the bay leaf and 600ml/1 pint/2½ cups of the reserved stock. Transfer the casserole to the oven and braise for 30 minutes.

6 Meanwhile, place the tentacles in an ovenproof dish, pour the remaining olive oil over them and heat through in the oven. Combine with the rice mixture before serving.

MEAT & POULTRY

Pork, goat, partridge, woodcock and rabbit are some of the meat and game favoured by the Portuguese. In this chapter you will find an enticing variety of succulent stewed, braised and roasted dishes.

MANY LOCAL MEAT SPECIALITIES from Portugal are now exported to other countries – including the classic smoked sausages and other cuts made of Bisaro pork, a semi-wild pig from the north, and "black" pork, from a dark-skinned pig fattened on acorns, from the south.

Pork is the most popular meat. The tradition of keeping a pig or two for home consumption still exists in rural areas, and there are many recipes for all the different cuts, including home-made sausages and even tripe, made from the pig's stomach. Goat meat is also popular in the centre and north, where the mountainous landscape suits this nimble-footed animal. Sheep are raised for meat over the whole country, and veal production is now spreading from the north as far as the Alentejo, the central southern plains.

All kinds of meat are braised slowly in the oven, particularly cuts that need long, gentle cooking. These dishes were traditionally made in a wood-fired oven, which had first been raised to a high temperature to bake bread. As the oven cooled, the meat dishes were left to stew slowly in a wine and onion sauce with some herbs and spices, as in *carrilheira de porco preto em vinho tinto com cominhos* (pork in red wine with cumin). The longer the cooking, the more juice is released from the meat and vegetables, giving a wonderfully succulent texture to the meat.

The Portuguese prefer free-range chickens with strong-tasting meat. In rural areas, it is normal to keep chickens for the pot and there might be several in each backyard, a great source of eggs and meat for even the poorest. All the parts of the chicken are eaten, as with pork – even the blood is sometimes added to a stew to flavour it. Rice is a favourite accompaniment to a chicken stew, and is best cooked in the broth.

Enterprising Portuguese cooks have also devised many recipes for game, a source of free meat for the country-dweller. Many of these wild birds and animals, such as partridge, woodcock, hare and rabbit, would be marinated in the local wine and braised gently in the oven to tenderize them and release their strong flavour.

SERVES 4

1kg/2¼ lb pork ribs, cut into 2cm/¾ in slices

3 garlic cloves, chopped

1 litre/1¾ pints/4 cups olive oil

2 bay leaves

sea salt

For the *milhos*

50ml/2fl oz/¼ cup olive oil

1 onion, finely chopped

2 ripe tomatoes, peeled and cut into quarters

750ml/1¼ pints/3 cups chicken stock or water

250g/9oz/2¼ cups coarse cornmeal

COOK'S TIP

Serve the *milhos* as soon as it becomes creamy, as otherwise it tends to thicken.

VARIATION

To make the *milhos* richer, you can add some turnip tops, cut into thin slices, when you add the tomatoes.

PER PORTION Energy 1035kcal/4304kJ; Protein 53.2g; Carbohydrate 48.4g, of which sugars 2.4g; Fat 69.5g, of which saturates 17.9g; Cholesterol 165mg; Calcium 47mg; Fibre 2.1g; Sodium 250mg.

ROAST PORK RIBS WITH *MILHOS*
ENTRECOSTO ASSADO COM MILHOS

It may sound inappropriate to cook fatty meat in a lot of olive oil, but this produces excellent results, because the meat becomes smooth and the fat reduces. *Milhos*, the Portuguese equivalent of polenta, is prepared all over the country, including the Madeira islands, with different regional textures and flavours. If coarse cornmeal is used, the results are usually a little more liquid than with fine cornmeal. All kinds of ingredients may be added, including meat, fish or vegetables, but also sweet versions are popular and cinnamon, milk and honey are used to cook simple but tasty desserts.

1 Preheat the oven to 140°C/275°F/Gas 1. Place the meat on a baking tray or in a shallow ovenproof dish about 5cm/2in deep. Season with salt and sprinkle with the garlic, then pour over the olive oil. Roast for about 2 hours.

2 Towards the end of the roasting time, prepare the *milhos*. Heat the oil in a large pan. Add the onion and cook over a low heat, stirring occasionally, for 5–10 minutes, until the onion is softened and translucent. Add the tomatoes and cook for a few more minutes.

3 Add 500ml/17fl oz/generous 2 cups of the stock or water and bring to the boil. Sprinkle in the cornmeal, whisking constantly. As the mixture starts to thicken, add the remaining stock. Season to taste with salt, but if you are using stock rather than water, you will probably not need any. Simmer for about 3 minutes, until creamy.

4 Remove the meat from the oven, place on a dish and serve immediately, handing round the *milhos* separately at the table.

GRILLED PORK WITH TURNIP TOPS AND BLACK-EYED BEANS

LOMBINHO DE PORCO GRELHADO COM MIGAS DE GRELOS E FEIJÃO FRADE

This mixture of turnip tops and beans makes an excellent accompaniment to grilled meat. The light, bitter taste of the vegetable makes a delicious contrast to the succulent meat. This dish is frequently eaten in the centre and north of Portugal and the grilled pork is often combined with bean stews.

1 If using uncooked beans, soak them overnight. Cook in a pan with water for an hour, drain and set aside.

2 Preheat the grill (broiler) to high. Cook the turnip tops in salted boiling water for a few minutes, being careful not to overcook them. Drain well, refresh in iced water, drain again and squeeze as dry as possible. Slice thinly with a sharp knife.

3 Season the pork on both sides with salt and place on the grill rack. Cook for 2 minutes on each side, then lower the heat and cook, turning once, for a further 8 minutes, until the pork is cooked through and tender. Leave to rest for another 5 minutes in a warm place to allow the inside temperature to stabilize.

4 Heat the olive oil in a pan. Add the turnip tops, beans and garlic and cook over a low heat for 5 minutes. Stir in the breadcrumbs and cook for a few minutes more. Transfer the pork fillets to warm plates and serve immediately with the vegetables.

SERVES 4

150g/5oz/scant 1 cup uncooked black-eyed beans, or 250g/9oz/scant 1½ cups black-eyed beans (peas), cooked

500g/1¼ lb turnip tops

4 pork fillets, preferably from black pork, weighing about 175g/6oz each

105ml/7 tbsp olive oil

2 garlic cloves, chopped

100g/3¾ oz/generous 1¾ cups breadcrumbs, made from corn bread

sea salt

VARIATIONS

• You can use the same quantity of spinach instead of the turnip tops.

• Instead of the beans, you can use potatoes, boiled in their skins and then peeled.

PER PORTION Energy 604kcal/2532kJ; Protein 49.8g; Carbohydrate 41.8g, of which sugars 7.2g; Fat 27.6g, of which saturates 5.3g; Cholesterol 110mg; Calcium 142mg; Fibre 9.5g; Sodium 338mg.

MEAT & POULTRY **89**

SERVES 4

50g/2oz/¼ cup plain (all-purpose) flour

800g/1¾ lb pork cheeks, preferably from black pork, cleaned and trimmed

50ml/2fl oz/¼ cup olive oil

2 onions, chopped

250ml/8fl oz/1 cup red wine

50ml/2fl oz/¼ cup ruby port

5ml/1 tsp ground cumin

2 bay leaves

sea salt

boiled potatoes, to serve

PER PORTION Energy 464kcal/1938kJ; Protein 45.3g; Carbohydrate 19.3g, of which sugars 7.4g; Fat 17.1g, of which saturates 4.1g; Cholesterol 126mg; Calcium 62mg; Fibre 1.8g; Sodium 148mg.

PORK CHEEKS STEWED IN RED WINE WITH CUMIN

CARRILHEIRA DE PORCO PRETO EM VINHO TINTO COM COMINHOS

Pork cheeks are ideal for slow cooking, and after an extended simmering process, they attain a juicy, gelatinous quality. Red wine and cumin complement each other to perfection, while the port smooths out the flavour. As an alternative to boiled potatoes, serve with mashed potatoes prepared with olive oil instead of butter and sprinkle with some lemon rind.

1 Spread out the flour on a plate. Add the pork cheeks and toss to coat, shaking off any excess. Heat half the olive oil in a large pan and cook over a medium heat, turning occasionally, for 5–10 minutes, until lightly coloured. Remove from the pan with a slotted spoon and reserve.

2 Discard the olive oil and wipe out the pan with kitchen paper. Add the remaining oil and heat. Add the onions and cook over a low heat, stirring occasionally, for 5 minutes, until translucent and softened.

3 Add the wine, port, cumin and bay leaves, return the pork cheeks to the pan and simmer gently for 15 minutes. Season with salt, cover and simmer for a further 2 hours. Serve with boiled potatoes.

PORK CONFIT WITH GREEN ASPARAGUS BREAD MASH

CARNE DE PORCO NO PINGUE COM MIGAS DE ESPARGOS VERDES

This is a speciality from Alentejo, in the south of Portugal. The green asparagus bread mash can also be made with other ingredients, such as tomatoes or wild herbs. Whatever ingredients are used, it is only when the mash achieves the shape of an omelette that it is ready.

1 Place the pork in a bowl. Mix together the paprika paste, wine, garlic and bay leaves, add to the pork and leave to marinate for 6 hours.

2 Melt the fat in a pan. Add the meat and cook over a low heat for 2 hours.

3 Meanwhile, prepare the mash. Cut off the crust from the bread and cut the bread into cubes.

4 Transfer 30ml/2 tbsp of the fat from the meat to a frying pan and heat. Add the bacon and garlic and cook, stirring occasionally, for about 5 minutes, until the bacon is lightly browned. Add the bread and 400ml/14floz/1⅔ cups water and blend well with a wooden spoon. You may have to add more water or fat to get a smooth texture like potato mash.

5 Add the asparagus and the coriander, and roll the mixture so that it forms the shape of an omelette.

6 Remove the meat with a slotted spoon and serve with the mash.

SERVES 4

700g/1lb 9oz pork shoulder, cut into 40g/1½oz cubes
60ml/4 tbsp paprika paste
50ml/2fl oz/¼ cup white wine
2 garlic cloves, chopped
2 bay leaves
1kg/2¼lb pork or duck fat
sea salt

For the green asparagus bread mash
800g/1¾lb day-old white bread
100g/3¾oz/generous ½ cup diced bacon
1 garlic clove, chopped
400g/14oz green asparagus, cooked
15ml/1 tbsp chopped fresh coriander (cilantro)

COOK'S TIP

Paprika paste is a sweet chilli marinade made with red paprika and salt commonly used as an ingredient in the Alentejo (south) and the Azores islands.

PER PORTION Energy 925kcal/3899kJ; Protein 63.5g; Carbohydrate 105.9g, of which sugars 7.2g; Fat 29.9g, of which saturates 9.4g; Cholesterol 135mg; Calcium 289mg; Fibre 4.7g; Sodium 1554mg.

SERVES 4

1kg/2¼ lb pork loin, preferably from black pork

15ml/1 tbsp sweet paprika

15ml/1 tbsp chopped fresh thyme

3 garlic cloves, finely chopped

105ml/7 tbsp white wine

105ml/7 tbsp olive oil

sea salt and ground black pepper

For the stew

50ml/2fl oz/¼ cup olive oil

1 onion, finely chopped

50g/2oz/⅓ cup bacon, finely diced

100g/3¾ oz wild mushrooms, such as ceps and horn of plenty, chopped

300g/11oz/scant 2 cups cooked chickpeas, plus 100ml/3½fl oz/scant ½ cup cooking liquid

100g/3¾ oz day-old white bread, crust removed, cut into cubes

1 small bunch of parsley, chopped

VARIATION

An alternative way to cook the pork is to cover it with pork or duck fat and roast in a preheated oven at 90ºC/ 195°F for 4 hours, then rinse and pat dry. Increase the oven temperature to 180°C/350°F/Gas 4, return the meat to the oven and cook for 20 minutes for a crispy outside. This cooking method is known as a confit.

BRAISED PORK AND CHICKPEA STEW WITH WILD MUSHROOMS
CACHAÇO DE PORCO ASSADO COM ENSOPADO DE GRÃO

Slow cooking that allows the meat to become tender and juicy on the inside and crisp on the outside is the secret of many superb Portuguese dishes, including this one. It also allows the fat in the meat to dry a little and bring flavour. The chickpea stew, which can be a meal in itself, combines well with the pork, and with other meat, such as game.

1 Trim off any excess fat from the pork and cut the meat into pieces weighing 125g/4¼ oz. Place them in a shallow, ovenproof dish. Mix together the paprika, thyme, garlic, wine and olive oil in a jug (pitcher), and season with salt and pepper. Pour the mixture over the meat, cover and leave to marinate for 4 hours.

2 Preheat the oven to 140°C/275°F/Gas 1. Place the dish in the oven with the marinade and braise for 2 hours.

3 Towards the end of the cooking time, prepare the chickpea stew. Heat the oil in a pan. Add the onion and bacon and cook over a low heat, stirring occasionally, for 5–8 minutes, until the onion has softened and the bacon is lightly coloured.

4 Add the mushrooms and cook for 5 minutes. Add the chickpeas, the reserved cooking liquid and the bread. Cook, stirring, until the bread has disintegrated, then add the parsley.

5 Remove the pork from the oven and serve immediately, with the chickpea stew.

PER PORTION Energy 756kcal/3155kJ; Protein 64.1g; Carbohydrate 26g, of which sugars 1.2g; Fat 42.8g, of which saturates 8.5g; Cholesterol 164mg; Calcium 89mg; Fibre 3.7g; Sodium 666mg.

SERVES 4

50ml/2fl oz/¼ cup olive oil

4 lamb shanks, about 275g/10oz each

4 onions, thinly sliced

2 garlic cloves, chopped

50ml/2fl oz/¼ cup white wine

1 bay leaf

1 *chouriço* sausage

125g/4¼oz bacon, cut into four pieces

2 carrots, sliced

125g/4¼oz green beans, cut into short lengths

2 turnips, diced

400g/14oz/2⅓ cups cooked chickpeas

salt

1 small bunch of mint, chopped, to garnish

COOK'S TIP

Take care when seasoning with salt, as sausage and bacon contain salt.

LAMB SHANK WITH CHICKPEAS, VEGETABLES AND SAUSAGES

PERNIL DE BORREGO COM COZIDO DE GRÃO

Lamb stews are widespread in central and southern Portugal. They differ slightly in the choice of spices, but the trick is to keep them simple. Slow cooking times are one of the secrets and it is also important to use a lot of thinly sliced onions, as well as black pepper, paprika, bay leaves and garlic to add flavour. After cooking, the onions will have become a juicy sauce.

1 Heat half the olive oil in a pan big enough to hold the lamb shanks. Add the lamb shanks and cook over a medium heat, turning occasionally, for 5–8 minutes, until lightly coloured. Remove them from the pan and reserve.

2 Discard the oil and wipe out the pan with kitchen paper. Place the remaining olive oil, the onions and garlic in the pan and return the lamb shanks. Add the white wine, bay leaf, sausage and bacon, then cover and cook over a low heat, stirring occasionally, for about 2 hours, until tender. Season with salt to taste.

3 Cook the carrots, green beans and turnips in salted boiling water until tender. Drain.

4 Remove the sausage from the pan and cut into 2cm/¾in slices. Return the sausage to the pan, add the vegetables and chickpeas, and cook for a further 5 minutes so that all the flavours blend. Transfer to a warm serving dish and garnish with the mint.

PER PORTION Energy 688kcal/2868kJ; Protein 39.3g; Carbohydrate 34.9g, of which sugars 11.8g; Fat 43.7g, of which saturates 14.6g; Cholesterol 115mg; Calcium 134mg; Fibre 7.9g; Sodium 1143mg.

ROASTED GOAT RIBATEJO-STYLE
CABRITO ASSADO À RIBATEJANA

Goat meat is a traditional ingredient in Portuguese cooking, but it can sometimes be hard to purchase in other countries. You could also use a leg of lamb – an average leg serves about three people and takes a little longer to cook than a shoulder.

1 Put the fat, garlic, sausage, paprika and white wine in a food processor, add a little salt and process until thoroughly combined. Spread this mixture over the meat and leave to stand for 2 hours.

2 Preheat the oven to 160°C/325°F/Gas 3. Place the meat on a roasting pan and roast for about 1½ hours.

3 Carve the meat into slices and serve with roast potatoes and spring onions.

SERVES 4

200g/7oz pork or duck fat

2 garlic cloves

1 small sausage, cut into cubes

5ml/1 tsp sweet paprika

50ml/2fl oz/¼ cup white wine

500g/1¼ lb saddle of goat, or 2 shoulders of goat or lamb, about 500g/1¼ lb each

sea salt

roasted baby potatoes and spring onions (scallions), to serve

PER PORTION Energy 711kcal/2959kJ; Protein 55.5g; Carbohydrate 0.1g, of which sugars 0.1g; Fat 55g, of which saturates 22.2g; Cholesterol 172mg; Calcium 14mg; Fibre 0g; Sodium 139mg.

SERVES 4

25g/1oz/2 tbsp butter

30ml/2 tbsp olive oil

4 fillet steaks (beef tenderloin), weighing about 175g/6oz each

30ml/2 tbsp mild mustard (preferably Savora)

105ml/7 tbsp single (light) cream

105ml/7 tbsp milk

juice of ½ lemon

sea salt

chips (French fries), to serve

COOK'S TIP

Savora is the kind of mustard used for this dish in Portugal. It is slightly sweet and a little spicy.

STEAK WITH MUSTARD SAUCE
BIFE À MARRARE

This steak was a key dish that was served in traditional coffee houses in Lisbon, where intellectuals and poets gathered. It is now strongly associated with the cuisine of Lisbon. The recipe is quite delicious, with plenty of sauce in which the potatoes can be submerged. The mustard used should not be overly spicy, but slightly sweet.

1 Melt the butter with the oil in a large frying pan. Season the steaks with salt, add to the pan and cook until done to your liking: about 2 minutes each side for rare and 3 minutes each side for medium. Remove the steaks from the pan and set aside. Discard the fat from the pan.

2 Put the mustard, cream, milk and lemon juice in the pan, add the steaks and heat gently, shaking the pan to blend well. Serve hot with chips.

PER PORTION Energy 475kcal/1976kJ; Protein 42.1g; Carbohydrate 2.6g, of which sugars 2.4g; Fat 33g, of which saturates 14.2g; Cholesterol 131mg; Calcium 70mg; Fibre 0g; Sodium 390mg.

SERVES 4

50ml/2fl oz/¼ cup olive oil

4 rib-eye steaks, each weighing about 240g/8½ oz

4 garlic cloves, lightly crushed

4 small bay leaves

120ml/4fl oz/½ cup white wine

8 slices of cured ham

sea salt

deep-fried potato slices or baked potatoes, to serve

PER PORTION Energy 539kcal/2246kJ; Protein 57.7g; Carbohydrate 4.5g, of which sugars 0.8g; Fat 30.2g, of which saturates 10g; Cholesterol 145mg; Calcium 21mg; Fibre 1g; Sodium 446mg.

RIB-EYE STEAK WITH HAM, GARLIC AND BAY LEAVES

BIFE DO ACÉM À PORTUGUESA

This is a classic steak recipe, traditionally prepared in a terracotta dish. If you have some beef stock available, add it to the sauce to make it richer. Rib-eye is a fantastic cut as its fat melts during cooking, flavouring the meat. Salt the meat immediately before frying, using sea salt instead of the refined variety, as it improves the taste.

1 Heat half the oil in a large pan. Lightly season the steaks with sea salt, add them to the pan and cook until done to your liking (use about 3 minutes each side for rare and 4 minutes each side for medium). Remove the steaks from the pan and keep them warm.

2 Add the remaining oil, the garlic and bay leaves, then pour in the wine and cook for a few minutes more.

3 Place the steaks on warm plates, top each with two slices of ham and spoon the sauce over them. Serve immediately, with the potatoes of your choice.

TRIPE STEWED PORTO-STYLE
TRIPAS À MODA DO PORTO

Porto has a culinary reputation for tripe. There is a legend that because explorers took all the meat supplies on their sailing trips, Porto was just left with tripe, so they were forced to invent recipes using this ingredient. This recipe is distinguished by the combination of the moist jelly of the calf's feet and the drier smoothness of the chicken.

1 Put the calf's feet in a very large pan with the bay leaves, half the parsley and the spiked onions and add water to cover. Bring to the boil, then lower the heat, cover and simmer for 20 minutes. Add the tripe, re-cover the pan and cook for a further 1–1¼ hours, until tender.

2 Transfer the tripe and feet to a board. Cut the tripe into wide strips and cut the meat off the foot bones. Reserve 750ml/1¼ pints/3 cups of the cooking liquid. Discard the remainder and the vegetables and herbs.

3 Heat the olive oil in a large pan. Add the chopped onions and garlic and cook over a low heat, stirring occasionally, for 5 minutes, until softened. Add the thyme and carrots and cook for a few minutes more. Pour in the port and cook until it has almost completely evaporated.

4 Add the sausage, ham, chicken, tripe strips and the meat from the calf's feet. Stir in the reserved cooking liquid, season with salt and pepper and simmer for about 20 minutes, until the chicken is cooked through and tender.

5 Chop the remaining parsley and add to the pan with the beans. Heat through gently and serve hot with rice.

SERVES 8

2 calf's feet, prepared and blanched
2 bay leaves
1 bunch of parsley
2 whole onions, each studded with 6 cloves
1.2kg/2½ lb tripe, prepared and blanched
50ml/2fl oz/¼ cup olive oil
2 onions, chopped
4 garlic cloves, chopped
1 small bunch of thyme, chopped
4 carrots, diced
75ml/5 tbsp white port
1 sausage, diced
150g/5oz cured ham, diced
8 chicken thighs
1kg/2¼ lb/5⅔ cups haricot beans, cooked
sea salt and ground black pepper
boiled rice, to serve

PER PORTION Energy 593kcal/2507kJ; Protein 58.7g; Carbohydrate 60.5g, of which sugars 6.9g; Fat 13.5g, of which saturates 3.8g; Cholesterol 180mg; Calcium 225mg; Fibre 20.4g; Sodium 496mg.

SERVES 6

1 free-range chicken, weighing about 1.8kg/4lb, cut into portions

2 garlic cloves, chopped

50ml/2fl oz/¼ cup white wine

sea salt

For the rice

800g/1¾ lb/5⅔ cups shelled broad (fava) beans, thawed if frozen

105ml/7 tbsp olive oil

2 onions, chopped

1 sausage with little fat or *salpicão*

1 bay leaf

750ml/1¼ pints/3 cups chicken stock

250g/9oz/1¼ cups long grain rice

PER PORTION Energy 823kcal/3429kJ; Protein 52.6g; Carbohydrate 50.9g, of which sugars 2.1g; Fat 45g, of which saturates 11.1g; Cholesterol 205mg; Calcium 104mg; Fibre 8.8g; Sodium 417mg.

BAKED CHICKEN WITH BROAD BEAN RICE

GALO ASSADO COM ARROZ DE FAVAS

This dish is a delightful combination of baked marinated chicken with juicy rice, broad beans and sausage. It should, ideally, be prepared with free-range chicken, which is much tastier and more tender. If the chicken is not free-range, reduce the cooking time by half.

1 Season the chicken portions with salt and place in an ovenproof dish. Sprinkle with the garlic, pour over the wine and leave to marinate for 2 hours.

2 Preheat the oven to 160°C/325°F/Gas 3. Cover the dish of chicken portions and bake in the oven for about 1½ hours, until cooked through and tender. Meanwhile, pop the beans out of their skins by squeezing gently between your finger and thumb.

4 About 55 minutes before the end of the chicken's cooking time, heat the olive oil in a pan. Add the onions and cook over a low heat, for 5 minutes, until softened. Add the sausage, bay leaf and 300ml/½ pint/1¼ cups of the stock and simmer for 30 minutes.

5 Remove the sausage and bay leaf from the pan. Discard the bay leaf, cut the sausage into small cubes and return it to the pan. Add the remaining stock and bring to the boil, then add the rice and cook for about 10 minutes.

6 Add the broad beans and cook for about 5 more minutes, until tender and still moist. Serve the chicken with the juicy rice handed round separately.

CHICKEN THIGHS WITH CABBAGE AND CHICKPEAS

COXA DE FRANGO COM PENCA E GRÃO

This meal is cooked in one pot and is particularly associated with central and northern Portugal. Its cooking method makes it ideal for serving to large numbers of people. The combination of meat with chickpeas and cabbage provides a nourishing dish. Sometimes pasta, such as penne, is added.

1 Heat the olive oil in a large pan. Add the onion and cook over a low heat, stirring occasionally, for 5 minutes, until softened. Increase the heat to medium, add the bacon, sausage, carrots, garlic, bay leaves, thyme sprigs and peppercorns and cook, stirring constantly, for a few minutes more.

2 Add the chicken, pour in enough water just to cover and season with salt. Bring just to the boil, then lower the heat, cover and simmer gently for 40 minutes. Remove the chicken and keep warm. Reserve the cooking liquid but remove and discard the bay leaves and thyme sprigs.

3 Meanwhile, prepare the cabbage. Cut in half and cut out the central hard part, then separate the leaves and cut into large slices. Cook in lightly salted boiling water for about 10 minutes. Drain well.

4 Mix the cabbage with the chickpeas, then add the reserved cooking liquid. Heat through and blend well, then serve the chicken with the vegetables.

SERVES 4

105ml/7 tbsp olive oil
1 onion, chopped
100g/3¾oz/generous ½ cup diced bacon
1 sausage, diced
3 carrots, diced
2 garlic cloves, chopped
2 bay leaves
2 thyme sprigs
8 black peppercorns
8 chicken thighs or 4 chicken legs
1 cabbage
250g/9oz/1½ cups cooked chickpeas
sea salt

PER PORTION Energy 456kcal/1894kJ; Protein 19.6g; Carbohydrate 23.6g, of which sugars 10.5g; Fat 32g, of which saturates 7g; Cholesterol 55mg; Calcium 126mg; Fibre 6.4g; Sodium 643mg.

SERVES 4

2 ducks, weighing about 1.8 kg/4lb each

5ml/1 tsp fresh rosemary leaves

50ml/2fl oz/¼ cup white port

100ml/4fl oz/½ cup olive oil

200g/7oz oyster mushrooms, sliced

100g/3¾oz/ generous ½ cup diced cured ham

100g/3¾oz/generous ½ cup diced bacon

2 garlic cloves, chopped

200g/7oz/1¾ cups black olives

sea salt and ground black pepper

cabbage and potatoes, to serve

VARIATIONS

• Another popular way to cook duck in Portugal is in the oven with rice. First, boil the duck with vegetables, sausage and a little red wine to make a tasty stock. Then put the duck meat and sliced sausage on a base of chopped onion and long grain rice and braise the ingredients in the stock for about 30 minutes – this is best done in a deep terracotta pot left uncovered, as this gives the dish an attractive brown colour on top. A little more stock may be needed during cooking, but only as much as is required to cook the rice without it becoming sloppy.

• Another dish using duck, from northern Trás-os-Montes, is a kind of fricassée of duck with cinnamon. The duck is cut into small pieces, braised in a covered dish, and then stewed with chopped onion. The sauce is then thickened with egg yolks and cinnamon.

PER PORTION Energy 643kcal/2686kJ; Protein 69.2g; Carbohydrate 2g, of which sugars 1.9g; Fat 38.5g, of which saturates 9.9g; Cholesterol 358mg; Calcium 73mg; Fibre 2g; Sodium 2143mg.

DUCK WITH BLACK OLIVES
PATO COM AZEITONAS

Easy to farm on a small scale in a peasant home, poultry, including duck, was considered a reliable and nutritious part of the traditional diet. This dish combines olives and mushrooms with duck. If you can't find white port, use brandy as an alternative, although port produces a subtler and more authentic flavour.

1 Bone the ducks, separating the legs and the breasts with the wings. Put the bones in a large pan with 50ml/2fl oz/½ cup of the olive oil and cook, turning frequently, for about 10 minutes, until coloured.

2 Season the duck meat with salt and pepper and sprinkle with the rosemary. Add to the pan and cook until lightly coloured. Pour in the port and enough water just to cover. Bring just to the boil, then lower the heat, cover and simmer for 30 minutes.

3 Remove the meat with a slotted spoon and reserve. Remove and discard the bones. Skim off the fat from the surface of the cooking liquid and reserve the liquid.

4 Preheat the oven to 200°C/400°F/Gas 6. Heat the remaining olive oil in a pan. Add the mushrooms, ham and bacon and cook over a low heat, stirring occasionally, for 5 minutes. Add the garlic, olives and the reserved cooking liquid.

5 Put the vegetable mixture in a terracotta or other ovenproof dish. Add the duck legs and breasts, skin side up, on top and place them, uncovered, in the oven for 15 minutes to dry a little and gain some colour. Serve immediately, with cabbage and potatoes.

PARTRIDGE IN MARINADE
PERDIZ DE ESCABECHE

Partridge is the favourite game bird of Portugal and it is commonly available throughout the country. It is usually cooked in a stew and each game hunter claims to have his own secret recipe. In the Douro region, which is the home of port wine, they like to marinate the bird in an intense ruby port before cooking. This recipe subtly enhances the natural flavour of the game. The dish can be served cold with a salad and bread, or alternatively served warm with potatoes.

1 Using poultry shears or strong kitchen scissors, cut the partridges in half. Place in a pan, add a little water and cook them for 3 minutes. Remove them from the pan and pat dry with kitchen paper, reserving the water.

2 Heat half the olive oil in a frying pan. Add the partridges and cook, turning occasionally, for about 10 minutes, until golden brown.

3 Meanwhile, heat the remaining oil in a large pan. Add the onions, garlic, carrot, bay leaves, black pepper and cloves and cook over a low heat, stirring occasionally, for 5 minutes.

4 Add the vinegar, wine and partridges to the pan. Add enough of the reserved cooking water to cover and then bring to the boil. Lower the heat, cover the pan and simmer for about 10 minutes. Season with salt and sprinkle with parsley. Remove from the heat and either serve straight away or leave to cool, transfer to a covered dish and store in the refrigerator for up to 2–3 days before eating cold.

SERVES 4

4 partridges
105ml/7 tbsp olive oil
2 onions, thinly sliced
2 garlic cloves, chopped
1 carrot, scraped and sliced lengthways
2 bay leaves
8–12 grains of black pepper
4 cloves
105ml/7 tbsp white wine vinegar
50ml/2fl oz/¼ cup white wine
1 small bunch of parsley, chopped
sea salt

VARIATIONS

• The onion base is integral to this recipe, but can be adapted using tomatoes, carrots, wild mushrooms, aubergine (eggplant) or bacon.
• Seasoning varies from region to region, but will often include both thyme and paprika.

PER PORTION Energy 938kcal/3919kJ; Protein 123.1g; Carbohydrate 12.3g, of which sugars 9.2g; Fat 43.4g, of which saturates 8.8g; Cholesterol 0mg; Calcium 218mg; Fibre 3g; Sodium 345mg.

WOODCOCK WITH MADEIRA
GALINHOLA COM MADEIRA

Woodcock is a small bird, weighing about 300g/11oz, so it is usual to allow one bird per serving. It is sometimes hard to get hold of, but is much prized for its flavour. Unlike other game birds, the innards, known as the "trail", are left intact apart from the gizzard – these are regarded as a great delicacy. This recipe gives quantities for each woodcock.

1 Clean the woodcock, rinse it and dispose of the gizzard. Season with salt and pepper and cover with the lard.

2 Place it in a pan with the onion and butter, and cook over a low heat for 30 minutes.

3 Remove the bird from the pan and remove the "trail". Mash it with the wine, then add to the sauce. Return the bird to the pan and cook for a further 10 minutes. Serve with fried bread and green beans.

SERVES 1

1 woodcock, or small pheasant
6 thin slices of lard
1 small onion, thinly sliced
90g/3½oz/scant ½ cup butter
50ml/2fl oz/¼ cup dry Madeira wine
sea salt and ground black pepper
fried bread and green beans, to serve

PER PORTION Energy 1204kcal/4985kJ; Protein 58.6g; Carbohydrate 6.5g, of which sugars 6.5g; Fat 98.8g, of which saturates 55.3g; Cholesterol 652mg; Calcium 78mg; Fibre 0g; Sodium 683mg.

SERVES 4

1 hare or rabbit, cleaned but with liver and blood reserved

105ml/7 tbsp olive oil

2 onions, chopped

100g/3¾oz/generous ½ cup diced bacon

1 green (bell) pepper, seeded and chopped

3 garlic cloves

3 carrots, diced

2 bay leaves

1 small bunch of thyme

150ml/¼ pint/⅔ cup white wine

600g/1lb 6oz/scant 4½ cups cooked haricot beans

1 small bunch of coriander (cilantro), chopped

30ml/2 tbsp chopped wild mint

sea salt

bread, to serve

PER PORTION Energy 586kcal/2454kJ; Protein 44.9g; Carbohydrate 33.4g, of which sugars 8.4g; Fat 28.6g, of which saturates 6.7g; Cholesterol 117mg; Calcium 150mg; Fibre 12.6g; Sodium 470mg.

HARE WITH WHITE BEANS

LEBRE COM FEIJÃO

In this traditional recipe from the Alentejo, the strong taste of the hare blends well with the absorbent texture of the white beans. The use of wild mint gives a notable, delicate freshness to the dish.

1 Cut the hare into 10 pieces – two forequarters, each hindquarter halved and the saddle cut into four pieces – and rinse. Reserve the liver and the blood.

2 Heat 45ml/3 tbsp of the olive oil in a large pan. Add the pieces of hare and cook, turning occasionally, for 5–10 minutes, until evenly browned. Remove the pieces of hare and set aside. Discard the olive oil.

3 Add the remaining oil to the pan and heat. Add the onions, bacon and green pepper and then cook over a low heat, stirring occasionally, for 5 minutes. Add the garlic and carrots and cook for a few minutes more.

4 Add the bay leaves, thyme, the reserved liver and blood, the wine and the pieces of hare. Add enough water just to cover and bring to the boil. Season with salt, lower the heat and simmer for about 1 hour, until the hare is tender.

5 Add the beans and cook for a further 5 minutes to heat through. Stir in the coriander and mint and serve with slices of bread.

DESSERTS & SWEET TREATS

The tempting delights featured in the following selection of recipes are defined by eggs, honey, sugar and butter. They offer both delicious snacks and sweet finales to your meals and include biscuits, cakes, pastries, sweet breads and desserts.

AND FINALLY, we reach the end of the meal. The Portuguese have a sweet tooth, and can usually find room for a dessert served before the cheese and coffee. Many traditional dessert recipes originated in the monasteries and convents throughout the country, where the monks and nuns devised tempting sweet pastries and desserts to sell to the townspeople.

It is the combination of ingredients that makes these desserts so Portuguese. The basics are sugar, eggs and flour. Next, the cook might add various nuts, fruits and spices, particularly cinnamon. Sometimes a yeast dough rather like a doughnut mixture is fried in batter and then drenched in sugar for *filhós*, or honey is added to a sponge pudding, which is then eaten with white ricotta cheese – *pudim de mel com requeijao batido*. Fruits are cooked in syrup and make a delicious topping on a base of sponge cake or pastry.

The Portuguese are very fond of their many kinds of bread, and they are used in sweet recipes as well as savoury. For a calorific dessert, bread is cut into strips, dipped into egg and fried, then topped with sugar and port wine sauce.

Best of all are the varieties of egg custard (*leite-creme*) and crème caramel (*pudim flan*), well sweetened and baked in the oven. They are spiced with cinnamon and vanilla, sometimes served in a pastry case, sometimes in unadorned splendour.

Rice is a favourite when used in sweet dishes as well as the more usual savoury ones, and the Portuguese version of rice pudding, *arroz doce*, appears at Christmas celebrations, as well as featuring on most restaurant menus. This decadent creamy pudding is well sweetened with sugar and sometimes dusted with elaborate patterns in cinnamon. A variant of this dessert, *aletria*, is based on vermicelli instead of rice.

In less busy days, when the well-to-do people of the big cities like Lisbon and Porto might have had more time on their hands, there were many tea shops where pastries and cakes such as *pasteis de nata* were eaten in the afternoons with a cup of tea. Nowadays, these pastries and cakes are more likely to surface at the end of a restaurant menu, or as part of a festive meal at New Year and Easter.

ALMOND BISCUITS
ARREPIADOS

These almond biscuits (cookies) perfectly complement both coffee and an after-supper glass of port. If you prefer them flatter, add some butter so that they drain while baking. Using roughly ground almonds gives the biscuits a crispier texture. Alternatively, make them with a mixture of hazelnuts and almonds, or just hazelnuts.

1 Preheat the oven to 180°C/350°F/Gas 4. Mix all the ingredients together until blended, using enough beaten egg to make a stiff paste. Shape into little balls.

2 Place the balls on a non-stick baking sheet, spaced well apart, and gently flatten them. Bake for about 10 minutes, until light brown. Leave to stand for 2 minutes, then transfer to a wire rack to cool completely.

MAKES 25

500g/1¼ lb/5 cups ground almonds
250g/9oz/generous 1 cup light brown sugar
5ml/1 tsp ground cinnamon
2–3 eggs, lightly beaten
grated rind of 1 lemon

PER BISCUIT Energy 168.4kcal/702.4kJ; Protein 4.8; Carbohydrate 11.9g, of which sugars 11.3g; Fat 11.6g, of which saturates 1g; Cholesterol 15.2mg; Calcium 56mg; Fibre 1.5g; Sodium 9.1mg.

MAKES ABOUT 20

6 eggs
150ml/¼ pint/⅔ cup olive oil
100g/3¾oz/generous ½ cup sugar
15ml/1 tbsp brandy
about 250g/9oz/2¼ cups plain (all-purpose) flour, plus extra for dusting

VARIATION

An alternative way of preparing these biscuits is to make the dough with more flour so it is less flexible, and then form small balls before baking them.

PER BISCUIT Energy 111.3kcal/464.8kJ; Protein 3g; Carbohydrate 9.7, of which sugars 0.2g; Fat 6.8g, of which saturates 1.2g; Cholesterol 57.1mg; Calcium 26mg; Fibre 0.4g; Sodium 21.4mg.

OLIVE OIL BISCUITS

BISCOITOS DE AZEITE

Olive oil is a natural resource in Portugal, and has an important role in the cuisine. Even sweet dishes, such as certain puddings and cakes, are prepared with olive oil. These biscuits (cookies) are another example.

1 Preheat the oven to 180°C/350°F/Gas 4. Beat the eggs with the olive oil, the sugar and brandy with an electric mixer until smooth.

2 Gradually beat in the flour on a low speed until a dough forms (you may not need all the flour).

3 Roll out the dough on a lightly floured surface and stamp out whatever shapes you like with a biscuit cutter.

4 Place on a non-stick baking sheet, spaced well apart, and bake for 10 minutes, until golden. Leave to stand for 2 minutes, then transfer to a wire rack to cool completely.

FLAT FRITTERS
FILHÓS

The paste for these flat fritters would traditionally have been made around the fire, with the grandmother teaching her grandchildren how to knead the paste in their hands using their knees for support. Then the fritters would have been cooked in a pan placed on a tripod over a few red-hot coals.

1 Heat the stock until it is just lukewarm. Place the yeast in a bowl and cream with 150ml/¼ pint/⅔ cup of the tepid stock. Set aside.

2 Sift the flour on to a marble slab or other cold work surface and make a well in the centre. Add the eggs and brandy to the well and gradually incorporate the flour with your hands, then add the yeast and stock mixture. Continue kneading the ingredients together, gradually adding more stock until the dough starts to loosen from the surface.

3 Shape the dough into a ball, cover with a clean dish towel and leave to rise in a warm place for about 1 hour. When the dough has risen, knock back (punch down). Grease your hands with oil. Take a small piece of the dough and flatten out into a round with a diameter of about 10cm/4in. Repeat with the remaining dough.

4 Heat the oil in a frying pan. Add the rounds, one or two at a time, and fry on both sides until puffed up and golden brown. Remove with a slotted spatula and drain on kitchen paper. When the fritters are cooked, sprinkle them with sugar and cinnamon and serve.

SERVES 8–12

300ml/½ pint/1¼ cups pumpkin stock (see Cook's Tip)
20g/¾ oz fresh yeast
1kg/2¼ lb/9 cups plain (all-purpose) flour
6 large (US extra large) eggs, lightly beaten
25ml/1½ tsp brandy
olive oil, for greasing and frying
sugar and ground cinnamon, for sprinkling

COOK'S TIP

Pumpkin stock is required both for this recipe and for "Dreams" (see opposite page). To make it, cook 1kg/2¼ lb/7¾ cups diced pumpkin in 2 litres/3½ pints/ 8¾ cups water with 5ml/1 tsp salt. Transfer to a food processor or blender and process to a purée, then pass through a sieve (strainer). The stock should have quite a thin consistency, so if it is too creamy, add some more water.

PER PORTION Energy 401kcal/1689kJ; Protein 11g; Carbohydrate 64.8g, of which sugars 1.3g; Fat 12.2g, of which saturates 2.1g; Cholesterol 95mg; Calcium 131mg; Fibre 2.6g; Sodium 38mg.

SERVES 8–10

750ml/1¼ pints/3 cups milk

20g/¾ oz fresh yeast

750g/1lb 10oz/6½ cups plain
(all-purpose) flour

8 eggs, lightly beaten

50ml/2fl oz/¼ cup brandy

750ml/1¼ pints/3 cups pumpkin stock

vegetable oil, for deep-frying

sugar and ground cinnamon, for sprinkling

PER PORTION Energy 439kcal/1850kJ; Protein 14.6g;
Carbohydrate 61.8g, of which sugars 4.7g; Fat 15.5g, of
which saturates 3.2g; Cholesterol 157mg; Calcium
218mg; Fibre 2.3g; Sodium 91mg.

DREAMS
SONHOS

The pumpkin stock gives a unique taste to these fried balls. They taste wonderful with a little sugar, especially when they are still warm from the oven. Dreams are traditionally made on Christmas Eve before the family gathers for the evening meal. A glass of tawny port is an excellent complement to this sweet dessert.

1 Heat the milk until just lukewarm. Cream the yeast with the tepid milk and set aside.

2 Sift the flour into a bowl and make a well in the centre. Add the eggs and gradually incorporate the flour, then add the milk mixture, brandy and pumpkin stock and mix well. The mixture should drop thickly from a spoon. Leave to rest for 30 minutes.

3 Heat the oil for deep-frying to 180–190°C/350–375°F or until a cube of day-old bread browns in 40 seconds. Stir the mixture again and, using two spoons, shape small pieces into little balls and place in the hot oil until browned. Remove with a slotted spoon, drain well, sprinkle with sugar and cinnamon and serve.

RINGS

ARGOLAS

These quirky-looking biscuits (cookies) are not baked, but deep-fried. In the small, rural villages of Portugal they would traditionally have been served on a table with a selection of other sweets to welcome visitors. On special occasions, they would have also been served and eaten as the village gathered around a big fire near the church.

1 Put all the ingredients, except the oil for deep-frying, in a large bowl and blend thoroughly. Shape the dough into a ball, cover and leave to rest for 30 minutes.

2 Grease your hands with olive oil, then break off small pieces of the dough and roll them between your palms to make "strings" of dough. Tie each "string" in a loose knot and place on a tray.

3 Heat the oil for deep-frying to 180–190°C/350–375°F or until a cube of day-old bread browns in 40 seconds. Add the knots to the hot oil, in batches, and deep-fry until golden brown. Remove with a slotted spatula and drain on kitchen paper.

SERVES 8

4 eggs
30ml/2 tbsp olive oil, plus extra for greasing
90g/3½ oz/½ cup sugar
50ml/2fl oz/¼ cup brandy
5ml/1 tsp salt
5ml/1 tsp dried yeast
1kg/2¼ lb/9 cups plain (all-purpose) flour
vegetable oil, for deep-frying

PER PORTION Energy 620kcal/2619kJ; Protein 14.9g; Carbohydrate 108.9g, of which sugars 13.6g; Fat 15.4g, of which saturates 2.6g; Cholesterol 95mg; Calcium 195mg; Fibre 3.9g; Sodium 285mg.

SERVES 12

melted butter, for brushing

40g/1½oz/¾ cup breadcrumbs, plus extra for sprinkling

200g/7oz/1¾ cups shelled almonds

500g/1¼ lb/generous 2¾ cups sugar

50g/2oz/¼ cup butter

4 eggs

6 egg yolks

icing (confectioner's) sugar, to decorate

PER PORTION Energy 364kcal/1529kJ; Protein 7.7g; Carbohydrate 47.3g, of which sugars 44.4g; Fat 17.4g, of which saturates 4.2g; Cholesterol 173mg; Calcium 88mg; Fibre 1.3g; Sodium 83mg.

ALMOND TART
TOUCINHO DO CÉU

Many varieties of this dessert, ranging in sweetness, are found all over Portugal. This recipe uses partly unpeeled almonds for additional flavour. The tart is made in two layers, a softer one on the base and a crunchier one on top. Serve with a raspberry sorbet and a lightly fresh tawny port.

1 Preheat the oven to 160°C/325°F/Gas 3. Brush a round cake tin (pan), 25cm/10in in diameter and 5cm/2in deep, with melted butter. Line with baking parchment and brush with melted butter again. Sprinkle with breadcrumbs, shaking out the excess.

2 Place half the almonds in a heatproof bowl and pour in boiling water to cover. Leave to stand for a few minutes, then drain and rub off the skins. Put all the almonds in a food processor and process until they have the texture of breadcrumbs.

3 Put the sugar in a pan, add 250ml/8fl oz/1 cup water and bring to the boil, stirring until the sugar has dissolved. Continue to boil, without stirring, until a thick syrup forms. Remove the pan from the heat and stir in the butter.

4 Mix together the eggs, egg yolks, almonds and breadcrumbs in a bowl, then stir into the syrup. Spoon the mixture into the prepared tin and bake for about 1 hour, until just firm but still moist. Turn out on to a rack to cool. Serve sprinkled with sifted icing sugar.

SPONGE CAKE
PÃO DE LÓ

There are many ways of preparing sponge cake and lots of villages have their own recipe, usually bearing the village's name. The differences are in the proportion of sugar, eggs and flour and – critically – the cooking time. This is a version from Ovar, located below Porto on the coast, which is also well known for its carnival. A very popular dish, it is distinctive for leaving the cake moist in the centre.

1 Preheat the oven to 160°C/325°F/Gas 3. Brush a round cake tin (pan), 20cm/8in in diameter and 5cm/2in deep, with melted butter. Line with baking parchment and brush with melted butter again.

2 Sift the flour into a bowl and set aside. Beat the eggs and yolks with the sugar in another bowl until light and fluffy. Gradually fold in the flour.

3 Spoon the mixture into the prepared tin and bake for 25 minutes. Leave to cool completely in the tin.

4 Meanwhile, make the cinnamon sauce. Put all the ingredients in a heatproof bowl. Set the bowl over a pan of barely simmering water and beat well until slightly thickened. Taste and beat in more cinnamon if required. Leave to cool.

5 To serve, remove the cake from the tin, using the baking parchment to ease it out. Cut into slices, bearing in mind that the centre is moist, and place on individual plates. Serve with the cinnamon sauce.

SERVES 6

melted butter, for brushing
125g/4¼oz/generous 1 cup plain (all-purpose) flour
6 eggs
12 egg yolks
240g/8½oz/generous 2 cups icing (confectioner's) sugar

For the cinnamon sauce
105ml/7 tbsp milk
45ml/3 tbsp icing (confectioner's) sugar
2 egg yolks
pinch of ground cinnamon

VARIATION

Melt 125g/4¼oz of bitter chocolate and 125g/4¼oz of butter in a bain-marie, and fold into the cake mixture at the end of step 2. Cook as before and freeze lightly before serving to produce a delightful chocolate sponge.

PER PORTION Energy 485kcal/2041kJ; Protein 15.8g; Carbohydrate 67.4g, of which sugars 51.5g; Fat 18.9g, of which saturates 5.4g; Cholesterol 662mg; Calcium 159mg; Fibre 0.7g; Sodium 102mg.

SERVES 8

250g/9oz/1¼ cups short grain rice
thinly pared rind of 1 lemon
1 cinnamon stick
pinch of salt
1.2 litres/2 pints/5 cups milk
150g/5oz/⅔ cup sugar
4 egg yolks
ground cinnamon, for sprinkling

SWEET RICE

ARROZ DOCE

This traditional dessert is a Christmas speciality that can also be prepared throughout the year. Pre-cooking the rice in water allows it to better absorb the milk and sugar during the cooking process. The rice is a similar shape to risotto rice, with a high amount of starch. The dish can also be made with a type of hair-thin pasta called *aletria*, often used in Portuguese cooking.

1 Put the rice, lemon rind, cinnamon stick and salt in a pan and pour in 500ml/17fl oz/ generous 2 cups water. Bring to the boil and simmer until almost dry.

2 Add 1 litre/1¾ pints/4 cups of the milk and the sugar to the pan with the rice and continue to cook, stirring frequently.

3 Meanwhile, mix the egg yolks with the remaining milk in a jug (pitcher). When the rice is beginning to become dry, stir in the egg yolk mixture. Remove the pan from the heat, pour the rice mixture into a tray and leave to cool and set.

4 Cut into squares and sprinkle with cinnamon. Serve in a deep plate.

PER PORTION Energy 286kcal/1203kJ; Protein 9g; Carbohydrate 51.6g, of which sugars 26.7g; Fat 5.5g, of which saturates 2.4g; Cholesterol 110mg; Calcium 208mg; Fibre 0g; Sodium 70mg.

FRIED BREAD WITH PORT SAUCE
RABANADAS

This is usually served as a winter treat. Although it originated as a way of using up day-old bread, it is so good that people deliberately choose to make it, buying bread and leaving it to become slightly stale just for this dish. It bears a passing resemblance to the children's favourite French toast or "eggy bread", but has a more sophisticated flavour.

1 Put the sugar, lemon rind and cinnamon stick in a pan, add the port and 200ml/ 7fl oz/scant 1 cup water and bring to the boil, stirring until the sugar has dissolved. Continue to boil, without stirring, for 3 minutes. Remove the pan from the heat and pour the syrup into a shallow, heatproof dish.

2 Beat the eggs in another shallow dish. Heat the oil for deep-frying to 180–190°C/ 350–375°F or until a cube of day-old bread browns in 30 seconds.

3 Meanwhile, briefly soak both sides of the bread slices first in the syrup and then in the egg. Add the slices to the hot oil, in batches, and deep-fry on both sides until golden brown. Remove with a slotted spatula and drain on a rack.

4 Strain the remaining syrup into a pan and boil for 5 more minutes. Serve the bread sprinkled with icing sugar and cinnamon, and hand the syrup separately.

SERVES 4

200g/7oz/scant 1 cup light brown sugar

thinly pared rind of 1 small lemon

1 cinnamon stick

50ml/2fl oz/¼ cup tawny port

4 eggs

vegetable oil, for deep-frying

8 slices of day-old white bread with crusts, about 2cm/¾in thick

icing (confectioner's) sugar and ground cinnamon, to serve

COOK'S TIP

Use a day-old white loaf with a diameter of about 7.5cm/3in, or a large ciabatta. Depending on the size of the bread, allow one or two slices per serving.

VARIATION

An alternative and easier way of using up day-old bread is to soak both sides of the bread briefly in milk and then deep-fry it. Serve sprinkled with sugar and cinnamon.

PER PORTION Energy 518kcal/2186kJ; Protein 11.1g; Carbohydrate 80.9g, of which sugars 55.2g; Fat 17.6g, of which saturates 2.8g; Cholesterol 190mg; Calcium 116mg; Fibre 0.8g; Sodium 360mg.

SERVES 12

600g/1lb 6oz/generous 3 cups sugar
50g/2oz/⅓ cup lard, cut into pieces
thinly pared rind of 1 small lemon
1 cinnamon stick
40ml/2½ tbsp tawny port
15 egg yolks

COOK'S TIPS

• This pudding is traditionally made in a single mould, similar in shape to a *kugelhopf* mould but with a lid. As it will be difficult to find, individual moulds are recommended here. If you do use a single mould, the pudding takes about 1 hour to bake.
• Liquid caramel is very hot and can burn badly. Be especially careful when pouring it into the moulds.

PER PORTION Energy 316kcal/1330kJ; Protein 3.9g; Carbohydrate 52.7g, of which sugars 52.7g; Fat 11g, of which saturates 3.6g; Cholesterol 256mg; Calcium 56mg; Fibre 0g; Sodium 15mg.

ABADE DE PRISCOS PUDDING
PUDIM ABADE DE PRISCOS

Abade de Priscos was the abbot of a small village, near Braga in the north of Portugal, who loved cooking. Even though it may look like caramel pudding, this dish uses different ingredients and has a much more subtle taste. It is prepared with a syrup instead of milk and sugar, and it is flavoured with port and lard, which give it its translucent texture. Serve in small portions because the flavour is intense.

1 Preheat the oven to 180°C/350°F/Gas 4. Put 200g/7oz/1 cup of the sugar in a pan and add 105ml/7 tbsp water. Bring to the boil, stirring until the sugar has dissolved, then continue to boil, without stirring, for 4–5 minutes, until it is a light caramel colour.

2 Pour a little of the caramel into a dariole mould, then, holding the mould with a cloth, swirl the caramel around to cover the sides. Pour the excess caramel into another mould and repeat the process until you have coated 12 moulds.

3 Place the remaining sugar in a pan and add 300ml/½ pint/1¼ cups water, the lard, lemon rind and cinnamon. Bring to the boil, stirring until the sugar has dissolved, then boil, without stirring, for about 7 minutes, until syrupy.

4 Strain into a bowl and blend in the port and egg yolks. Fill the moulds with the syrup custard and place them in a roasting pan.

5 Add boiling water to come about halfway up the sides of the moulds and bake for about 40 minutes, until just set.

ANGELS' CHEEKS WITH ORANGES

PAPOS DE ANJO COM LARANJA EM CALDA

This easy-to-prepare dessert is delightful served with oranges and raspberries, but will also go well with other fruits. As the "cheeks" are made without sugar, the sweetness comes from the fruit you serve them with. Many Portuguese desserts originated in convents, which explains the origin of the frequent religious references in the recipe names.

1 Wash the oranges thoroughly, then remove the rind with a citrus zester.

2 Put the orange rind and sugar in a pan and add 200ml/7fl oz/scant 1 cup water. Bring to the boil, stirring until the sugar has dissolved, then boil, without stirring for 5 minutes. Remove the pan from the heat.

3 Remove all the pith from the oranges and cut out the segments. Place in a heatproof bowl and add the syrup.

4 Preheat the oven to 160°C/325°F/Gas 3. Brush six ramekins, traditionally half-spheres measuring 70 x 35mm/3 x 1½in, with melted butter.

5 Beat the egg yolks and egg for about 10 minutes. Divide among the prepared ramekins, place in a tray with about 1cm/½in of warm water and bake for about 15 minutes, until golden. To serve, divide the oranges in syrup among individual plates, turn out an "angel's cheek" on top of each serving, and add a few raspberries.

SERVES 6

melted butter, for brushing
5 egg yolks
1 egg
24 raspberries, to serve

For the oranges in syrup
3 oranges
200g/7oz/1 cup sugar

PER PORTION Energy 217kcal/917kJ; Protein 4.3g; Carbohydrate 39.9g, of which sugars 39.9g; Fat 5.6g, of which saturates 1.6g; Cholesterol 200mg; Calcium 70mg; Fibre 1g; Sodium 24mg.

SERVES 8

olive oil, for brushing
breadcrumbs, for sprinkling
8 eggs
300g/11oz/1½ cups sugar
50g/2oz/2½ tbsp molasses
50g/2oz/¼ cup clear honey
2.5ml/½ tsp ground cinnamon
5ml/1 tsp dried yeast
ricotta or other fresh cheese, to serve

PER PORTION Energy 267kcal/1133kJ; Protein 7g; Carbohydrate 50.7g, of which sugars 48.2g; Fat 5.7g, of which saturates 1.6g; Cholesterol 190mg; Calcium 88mg; Fibre 0.1g; Sodium 108mg.

HONEY PUDDING WITH RICOTTA
PUDIM DE MEL COM REQUEIJÃO BATIDO

This recipe originated on the islands of Madeira and Azores, where similar versions are made. The flavour of this pudding is characterized by molasses. It is particularly delicious served with *requeijão*, a fresh cheese similar to ricotta, which provides an appealing contrast. It is also excellent accompanied by pumpkin marmalade.

1 Preheat the oven to 180°C/350°F/Gas 4. Brush eight 40cm/1½in square moulds with olive oil and sprinkle with breadcrumbs, shaking out the excess.

2 Beat the eggs in a bowl, then beat in all the remaining ingredients until well blended.

3 Divide the mixture among the prepared moulds and place them in a roasting pan. Add sufficient boiling water to come about halfway up the sides of the moulds and bake for about 15 minutes, until risen.

4 Give the puddings approximately 5 minutes to fully stabilise and then turn them out while they are still warm. Serve with ricotta or other fresh cheese.

SUPPLIERS

AUSTRALIA
Petersham, a suburb of
Sydney, also known as Little
Portugal, is full of Portuguese
butchers, delicatessens, cafés
and restaurants:

Quality Marine Seafood
65 New Canterbury Road
Petersham, Sydney
Tel: +61 02 9564 6900
Fresh seafood and bacalhau

Sweet Belem
35c New Canterbury Road
Petersham, Sydney
Tel: +61 02 9572 6685
Traditional cakes and breads

Talho Portuguese
95 New Canterbury Road
Petersham, Sydney
Tel: +61 02 9569 5552
Delicatessen

CANADA
Cafe Ferreira
1446 Peel Street
Montreal, QC H3A 1S8
Tel: +1 514 848 0988

Sintra Fine Dining
588 College Street West
Toronto, ON M6G 1B3
Tel: +1 416 533 1106

PORTUGAL
Charcutaria Brasil
Rua Alexandre Herculano 90
Lisbon 1250-012
Tel: +351 1 21 388 5644
Delicatessen

Manuel Tavares
Rua da Betesga, No 1A and 1B
1100-090 Lisbon
Tel: + 351 21 342 42 09

Pastéis de Belém
Rue de Belém, No 84 and 92
1300-085 Lisbon
Tel: +351 21 363 74 23
Cake shop

SOUTH AFRICA
Bembom, Comaro Crossing
Cnr. Comaro Street & Boundary
Road, Oakdene
Tel: +27 11 435 3618
Bakery and coffee shop

The Lusito Land Festival
Regents Park 2197
Johannesburg
Tel: +27 11 082 748 4840
Festival during April and May

The Portuguese Fish Market,
Restaurant, Deli & Sushi Bar
4a 7th Street, Melville
Johannesburg
Tel: +2711 726 3801

UNITED KINGDOM
A & C Co. Continental Groceries
3 Atlantic Road
London SW9 8HX
Tel: +44 20 7733 3766
Portuguese specialities

Armorica
19 Rams Walk, Petersfield
Hants GU32 3JA
www.armorica.co.uk
Online cookware retailer

Atlantico UK Ltd
Unit 10, Commerce Park
Croydon CR0 4ZS
Tel: +44 20 8649 7444
www.atlantico.co.uk
Portuguese food and drinks

Funchal Patisserie
141 Stockwell Road
London SW9 9TN
Tel: +44 20 7733 3134
www.funchal.ltd.uk
Portuguese bakery

Lisboa Delicatessen
54 Golborne Road
London W10 5NR
Tel: +44 20 8969 1052
Portuguese delicatessen

Original Fisherman
23 Electric Avenue
London SW9 8JP
Tel: +44 20 7733 3430
Fishmonger

Sharon and Chris Peacock
Cockerham Boers, Cockerham
Lancaster LA2 0ER
Tel +44 7947 026849
info@goat-meat.co.uk
Goat meat

UNITED STATES
Alcofa.com
Tel: +1 (973) 466 3480
www.alcofa.com
Online supermarket

Amaral's
www.amarals.com
Online retailer

Gourmet Foodstore
Tel: +1 (877) 591 8008
www.gourmetfoodstore.com
Online retailer

Nata's Pastries
13317 Ventura Blvd. # D
Sherman Oaks, CA 91423
Tel: +1 (818) 788 8050
www.nataspastries.com
Portuguese bakery

Porto Express
P.O. Box 484, Draper,
Utah 84020
admin@portoexpress.com
www.portoexpress.com
Online supermarket

Portuguese Bakery
2082 El Camino Real, Santa
Clara, CA 95050-4055
Tel: +1 (408) 984 2234
www.portuguesebakery.com
*Freshly made breads and
pastries*

Portuguesefood.com
Tel: +1 (508) 679 9830
www.portuguesefood.com
Online supermarket

Portugal Imports
11655 Artesia Blvd
Artesia CA 90701
Tel: +1 (562) 809 7021
www.portugalimportsofamerica.
com
*Wholesaler of Portuguese
goods, including freshly baked
breads and pastries*

INDEX

PUBLISHER'S ACKNOWLEDGEMENTS
We would like to thank the following for permission to reproduce their
images (t=top, b=bottom, r=right, l=left): p6 Jon Arnold Images/Alamy;
p7r JL Images/Alamy; p8 Stockfolio/Alamy; p9l Bob Krist/Corbis; p9r
Jose Pedro Fernandes/Alamy; p10l Charles Jean Marc/Corbis Sygma;
p10r Owen Franken/Corbis; p11 Peter Horree/Alamy; p12 Charles
O'Rear/Corbis; p13t Tony Arruza/Corbis; p13b Danita Delimont/Alamy;
p14t Keven Foy/Alamy; p14b Stephanie Maze/Corbis; p15 Charles
O'Rear/Corbis. All other photographs © Anness Publishing Ltd